D1302158

CCNA Command Quick Reference

Scott Empson

Cisco Press

800 East 96th Street
Indianapolis, IN 46240 USA

CCNA Command Quick Reference

Scott Empson

Copyright© 2005 Cisco Systems, Inc.

Cisco Press logo is a trademark of Cisco Systems, Inc.

Published by:
Cisco Press
800 East 96th Street
Indianapolis, IN 46240 USA

Printed in the United States of America   6 7 8 9 0

Sixth Printing: October 2008

Library of Congress Cataloging-in-Publication Number: 2004116146

ISBN: 1-58713-159-5

Warning and Disclaimer

This book is designed to provide information about the Certified Cisco Networking Associate (CCNA) exam and the commands needed at this level of Network Administration. Every effort has been made to make this book as complete and as accurate as possible, but no warranty or fitness is implied.

The information is provided on an "as is" basis. The authors, Cisco Press, and Cisco Systems, Inc. shall have neither liability nor responsibility to any person or entity with respect to any loss or damages arising from the information contained in this book or from the use of the discs or programs that may accompany it.

The opinions expressed in this book belong to the author and are not necessarily those of Cisco Systems, Inc.

Feedback Information

At Cisco Press, our goal is to create in-depth technical books of the highest quality and value. Each book is crafted with care and precision, undergoing rigorous development that involves the unique expertise of members from the professional technical community.

Readers' feedback is a natural continuation of this process. If you have any comments regarding how we could improve the quality of this book, or otherwise alter it to better suit your needs, you can contact us through e-mail at feedback@ciscopress.com. Please make sure to include the book title and ISBN in your message.

We greatly appreciate your assistance.

CISCO SYSTEMS

Corporate and Government Sales

Cisco Press offers excellent discounts on this book when ordered in quantity for bulk purchases or special sales.

For more information please contact: U.S. Corporate and Government Sales
1-800-382-3419 corpsales@pearsontechgroup.com

For sales outside the U.S. please contact: International Sales international@pearsoned.com

Trademark Acknowledgments

All terms mentioned in this book that are known to be trademarks or service marks have been appropriately capitalized. Cisco Press or Cisco Systems, Inc. cannot attest to the accuracy of this information. Use of a term in this book should not be regarded as affecting the validity of any trademark or service mark.

Publisher	John Wait
Editor-in-Chief	John Kane
Cisco Representative	Anthony Wolfenden
Cisco Press Program Manager	Jeff Brady
Executive Editor	Mary Beth Ray
Production Manager	Patrick Kanouse
Senior Development Editor	Christopher Cleveland
Copy Editor	Keith Cline
Technical Editors	Gerlinde Brady, David Kotfila
Team Coordinator	Tammi Barnett
Book and Cover Designer	Louisa Adair
Composition	Mark Shirar

CISCO SYSTEMS

Corporate Headquarters
Cisco Systems, Inc.
170 West Tasman Drive
San Jose, CA 95134-1706
USA
www.cisco.com
Tel: 408 526-4000
800 553-NETS (6387)
Fax: 408 526-4100

European Headquarters
Cisco Systems International BV
Haarlerbergpark
Haarlerbergweg 13-19
1101 CH Amsterdam
The Netherlands
www-europe.cisco.com
Tel: 31 0 20 357 1000
Fax: 31 0 20 357 1100

Americas Headquarters
Cisco Systems, Inc.
170 West Tasman Drive
San Jose, CA 95134-1706
USA
www.cisco.com
Tel: 408 526-7660
Fax: 408 527-0883

Asia Pacific Headquarters
Cisco Systems, Inc.
Capital Tower
168 Robinson Road
#22-01 to #29-01
Singapore 068912
www.cisco.com
Tel: +65 6317 7777
Fax: +65 6317 7799

Cisco Systems has more than 200 offices in the following countries and regions. Addresses, phone numbers, and fax numbers are listed on the
Cisco.com Web site at www.cisco.com/go/offices.

Argentina • Australia • Austria • Belgium • Brazil • Bulgaria • Canada • Chile • China PRC • Colombia • Costa Rica • Croatia • Czech Republic Denmark • Dubai, UAE • Finland • France • Germany • Greece • Hong Kong SAR • Hungary • India • Indonesia • Ireland • Israel • Italy Japan • Korea • Luxembourg • Malaysia • Mexico • The Netherlands • New Zealand • Norway • Peru • Philippines • Poland • Portugal Puerto Rico • Romania • Russia • Saudi Arabia • Scotland • Singapore • Slovakia • Slovenia • South Africa • Spain • Sweden Switzerland • Taiwan • Thailand • Turkey • Ukraine • United Kingdom • United States • Venezuela • Vietnam • Zimbabwe

About the Author

Scott Empson is currently an instructor in the Department of Telecommunications at the Northern Alberta Institute of Technology in Edmonton, Alberta, Canada, where he is tasked to teach Cisco routing, switching, and network design courses in a variety of different programs—certificate, diploma, and applied degree—at the post-secondary level. Scott is also the Program Coordinator of the Cisco Networking Academy Program at NAIT, a Regional Academy covering Central and Northern Alberta. He has earned three undergraduate degrees: a bachelor of arts, with a major in English; a bachelor of education, again with a major in English/language arts; and a bachelor of applied information systems technology, with a major in network management. He currently holds several industry certifications, including CCNP, CCDA, CCAI, and Network+. Prior to instructing at NAIT, he was a junior/senior high school English/language arts/computer science teacher at different schools throughout Northern Alberta. Upon completion of this project he plans to complete a master's degree. Scott lives in Edmonton, Alberta, with his wife and two children.

About the Technical Reviewers

Gerlinde Brady, M.A., CCNP has been a Cisco Certified Academy Instructor (CCAI) since 2000. She holds an M.A. degree in education from the University of Hanover, Germany. Besides A+ certification courses and general IT courses, she has been teaching Cisco CCNA and CCNP courses at Cabrillo College since 1999. Her industry experience includes LAN design, network administration, and technical support.

David Kotfila is the director of the Cisco Networking Academy Program at Rensselaer Polytechnic Institute (RPI) in Troy, New York. He is also on the National Advisory Council for the Networking Academy. In the past three years, more than 260 students have received their CCNA, and 80 students their CCNP at RPI. Previously, David was the senior manager in charge of training at PSINet, a Tier 1, global, Internet service provider. David enjoys spending time with his family, hiking in the mountains, and kayaking.

Dedications

To my wife, Trina, and my kids, Zachariah and Shaelyn. You are my meaning and purpose, and I love you all.

Acknowledgments

Wow, where do I begin? This book was not just me; it took a lot of people a lot of hours to put this all together in the form you see it now. So I guess a big thanks goes out to everyone at Cisco Press for making this all happen—Mary Beth Ray, Raina Han, and Chris Cleveland.

Thanks to my technical reviewers—Gerlinde Brady and David Kotfila—who corrected me when I was wrong or heading down the wrong path. Your dedication to your students and to the Cisco Networking Academy Program is obvious; your students are very fortunate to have you both as instructors.

Thanks to some former students of mine, both Academy and not—Wing, Lars, Brian, Mike, and Kyle—who reviewed some (very) rough drafts of this book and told me what worked and what didn't from a student's perspective. Good luck with the rest of your studies.

Special thanks go out to Terry Short, Chad Klymchuk, Colin Polanski, and Hans Roth for all of their advice and suggestions. Your students are also very fortunate to have you as instructors

Finally, a big note of thanks to William McBride and Randy Hirose for pushing me to do this.

Contents at a Glance

Contents

Icons Used in This Book

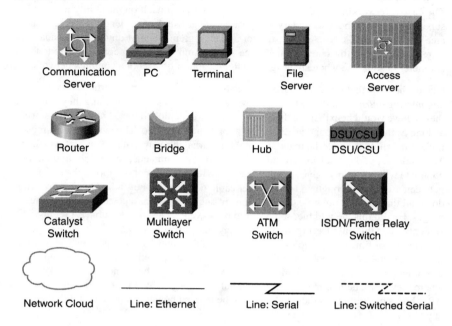

Command Syntax Conventions

The conventions used to present command syntax in this book are the same conventions used in the IOS Command Reference. The Command Reference describes these conventions as follows:

- **Boldface** indicates commands and keywords that are entered literally as shown. In actual configuration examples and output (not general command syntax), boldface indicates commands that are manually input by the user (such as a **show** command).

- *Italics* indicate arguments for which you supply actual values.

- Vertical bars (I) separate alternative, mutually exclusive elements.

- Square brackets [ ] indicate optional elements.

- Braces { } indicate a required choice.

- Braces within brackets [{ }] indicate a required choice within an optional element.

Introduction

The Cisco Networking Academy Program has long prided itself on the ability to provide superior training to both secondary and post-secondary students around the world in the area of CCNA and CCNP. As an instructor in the program here in Edmonton, Canada, it is so rewarding to use this curriculum and see students move from someone afraid to touch a computer to someone who can design, configure, and troubleshoot a complex network.

One of the tools that I use, as do many other Networking Academy instructors, is the *engineering journal*. I tell my students to write down in this journal anything they want that they believe would help them in their jobs as network administrators. Anything is allowed, as long as the notes are handwritten and not machine generated. This way students must review and study the material to put in into their journal in a way that is meaningful to them. The students put down all sorts of information: router commands; sample configurations, complete with diagrams; tables of which cables to use in different situations; the difference between a straight-through and a crossover cable. I even had one student attempt to write down all the different possible combinations of subnet masks and corresponding address ranges. He did this, he told me, so he would not have to learn how to subnet. I let my students carry this engineering journal into any sort of practical exam; if they have spent any amount of time on their journal, it can prove quite handy in a stressful period. During a practical final exam, I looked at this one student's journal, looking for the pages and pages of subnet mask/address combinations. They were nowhere to be found. When I asked him where they were, he told me that he ripped out those pages, because he didn't need them. After hours of writing out the combinations, he learned how to subnet and didn't them anymore!

So that is what this book is—an engineering journal that is cleaned up and definitely easier to read than my own poor handwriting. It is a summary of commands that are used at the CCNA level, following the format of the Cisco Networking Academy Program. But that is not to say that the only people who will find value in this book are Networking Academy students. Anyone preparing for the CCNA exam, or who needs to remember or review a command, will find this book relevant.

My reasons for writing this book are in response to comments made to me by two other Networking Academy instructors, William McBride and Randy Hirose. These two gentlemen were on course with me for the Instructor's CCNP 4 course in the Networking Academy. Whenever I needed to refresh my memory, I would go to look at my own personal engineering journals, but I could never find them; William or Randy had them. I would bug them to build their own, because that is what we tell our students to do, but they would laugh and say, "Publish this one, and I'll buy it." Bill and Randy—I did my part, now it's your turn!

Networking Devices Used in the Preparation of This Book

When working on this book, I tried to use devices that would be found in a majority of the Networking Academies. The Cisco Network Academy Program has been around for a few years now, and therefore there have been different devices used in Academy labs. Although

I was not able to test and confirm the commands on all of the routers and switches that Networking Academies have used, I did use the following equipment:

- C1720 router running Cisco IOS Software Release 12.0(1)XA3, with a fixed Fast Ethernet interface, and a WIC-2A/S serial interface card
- C2501 router running Cisco IOS Software Release 11.0(10c)XB1, with a fixed Ethernet interface, and two fixed serial interfaces
- C2620 router running Cisco IOS Software Release 12.0(7)T, with a fixed Fast Ethernet interface, a WIC-2A/S serial interface card, and a NM-1E Ethernet interface
- WS-C1912-EN Catalyst switch, running Enterprise Edition software
- WS-C2912-XL Catalyst switch, running version 12.0(5.3)WC(1) Enterprise Edition software
- WS-C2950-12 Catalyst switch, running version C2950-C3.0(5.3)WC(1) Enterprise Edition software

These devices were not running the latest and greatest versions of IOS. Some of it is quite old.

Those of you familiar with Cisco devices will recognize that a majority of these commands work across the entire range of the Cisco product line. These commands are not limited to the platforms and IOS versions listed. In fact, these devices are in most cases adequate for someone to continue their studies into the CCNP level as well.

Who Should Read This Book

This book is for those people preparing for the CCNA exam, whether through the Cisco Networking Academy Program or through some other means. But for those of you in the Networking Academy, this book follows the modules of the four courses of the CCNA Program, allowing you a quick reference to commands learned in each module. There are also some handy hints and tips along the way to hopefully make life a bit easier for you in this endeavor. It is also small enough that you will find it easy to carry around with you. Big heavy textbooks might look impressive on your bookshelf in your office, but can you really carry them all around with you when you are working in some server room or equipment closet somewhere?

Organization of This Book

This book follows the order of topics in the four CCNA courses of the Cisco Networking Academy Program. As it is meant to be a command summary guide, there is little content coming from CCNA 1—Networking Basics; the most important topic from this course is subnetting, which you will find in Appendix A. Otherwise, the book follows the Networking Academy curriculum, starting with CCNA 2, "Routers and Routing Basics," moving into CCNA 3, "Switching Basics and Intermediate Routing," and finishing with CCNA 4, "WAN Technologies." There are two appendixes: one on subnetting, the other on variable-length subnet masking (VLSM).

Specifically, the topics are as follows:

- **CCNA 2 Module 1, "WANs and Routers"**—An overview of how to connect to Cisco devices, which cables to use for which interfaces, and how to verify your IP settings using different operating systems.

- **CCNA 2 Module 2, "Introduction to Routers"**—How to navigate through the Cisco IOS; IOS editing commands, keyboard shortcuts, and IOS help commands.

- **CCNA 2 Module 3, "Configuring a Router"**—Commands needed to configure a single router: names, passwords, configuring interfaces, MOTD banners, IP host tables, saving and erasing your configurations.

- **CCNA 2 Module 4, "Learning About Other Devices"**—Commands related to CDP and about using Telnet to remotely connect to other devices.

- **CCNA 2 Module 5, "Managing Cisco IOS Software"**—Boot commands for the IOS; backing up and restoring IOS using TFTP and Xmodem; password recovery procedure for routers.

- **CCNA 2 Module 6, "Routing and Routing Protocols"**—How to configure static routes in your internetwork.

- **CCNA 2 Module 7, "Distance Vector Routing Protocols"**—Commands on configuring and verifying RIP and IGRP; how to see and clear your routing table.

- **CCNA 2 Module 8, "TCP/IP Suite Error and Control Messages"**—ICMP redirect commands.

- **CCNA 2 Module 9, "Basic Router Troubleshooting"**—Various **show** commands used to view the routing table.

- **CCNA 2 Module 10, "Intermediate TCP/IP"**—Turning on web servers on a router; the **netstat** command.

- **CCNA 2 Module 11, "Access Control Lists (ACLs)"**—Configuring standard ACLs; wildcard masking; creating extended ACLs; creating named ACLs; verifying ACLs.

- **CCNA 3 Module 1, "Introduction to Classless Routing"**—Configuring and verifying RIP-2; the IP subnet-zero command.

- **CCNA 3 Module 2, "Single-Area OSPF"**—Configuring and verifying single-area OSPF.

- **CCNA 3 Module 3, "EIGRP"**—Configuring and Verifying EIGRP.

- **CCNA 3 Module 4, "Switching Concepts"**—There are no commands affiliated with this module.

- **CCNA 3 Module 5, "Switches"**—There are no commands affiliated with this module.

- **CCNA 3 Module 6, "Switch Configuration"**—Commands needed for configuration of Catalyst 1900/2900/2950 switches: names; passwords, IP addresses, and default gateways; port speed and duplex; configuring static MAC addresses; managing the MAC address table; port security; password recovery procedures; firmware upgrades.

- **CCNA 3 Module 7, "Spanning Tree Protocol"**—Verifying spanning tree; setting switch priorities.

- **CCNA 3 Module 8, "Virtual LANs"**—Configuring static VLANs on 1900/2900/2950 switches; troubleshooting VLANs; saving and deleting VLAN information.

- **CCNA 3 Module 9, "VLAN Trunking Protocol"**—Configuring a VLAN Trunk Link; VTP configuration; verifying VTP; inter-VLAN communication; router-on-a-stick and subinterfaces.

- **CCNA 4 Module 1, "Scaling IP Addresses"**—Commands relating to NAT and DHCP configuration and verification.

- **CCNA 4, Module 2, "WAN Technologies"**—There are no commands affiliated with this module.

- **CCNA 4, Module 3, "PPP"**—Configuring PPP; authentication of PPP using PAP or CHAP; compression in PPP; multilink in PPP; troubleshooting PPP; returning to HDLC encapsulation.

- **CCNA 4, Module 4, "ISDN and DDR"**—Configuring a BRI interface; configuring a PRI interface; verifying ISDN; configuring legacy DDR; verifying and troubleshooting legacy DDR.

- **CCNA 4, Module 5, "Frame Relay"**—Configuring basic Frame Relay; Frame Relay and subinterfaces; DLCIs; verifying and troubleshooting Frame Relay.

- **CCNA 4, Module 6, "Introduction to Network Administration"**—Configuring SNMP; working with syslog.

- **Appendix A, "Subnetting"**—An overview of how to subnet; examples of subnetting a Class C and a Class B address; the Enhanced Bob Maneuver to subnetting.

- **Appendix B, "VLSM"**—An overview of VLSM; an example of using VLSM to make your IP plan more efficient.

Did I Miss Anything?

I am always interested to hear how my students do on both vendor exams and future studies. If you would like to contact me and let me know how this book helped you in your certification goals, please do so. Did I miss anything? Let me know. I can't guarantee I'll answer your e-mail message, but I can guarantee that I will read all of them. My e-mail address is ccnaguide@empson.ca.

There are no commands affiliated with the modules covered in CCNA 1 of the Cisco Networking Academy Program curriculum. However, please refer to Appendix A, "Subnetting," to ensure that you have a solid understanding of how to subnet. Your ability to quickly and correctly subnet can make a significant difference as to whether you fail or pass the CCNA exam.

PART II

CCNA 2

PART II CCNA 2

WANs and Routers

PART II CCNA 2

This chapter provides information and commands concerning the following topics:

- Connecting a rollover cable to your router or switch
- Determining what your terminal settings should be
- Understanding the setup of different LAN connections
- Identifying different serial cable types
- Determining which cable to use to connect your router or switch to another device
- Verifying IP settings depending on your operating system

Connecting a Rollover Cable to Your Router or Switch

Figure 1-1 shows how to connect a rollover cable from your PC to a router or switch.

Figure 1-1   Rollover Cable Connections

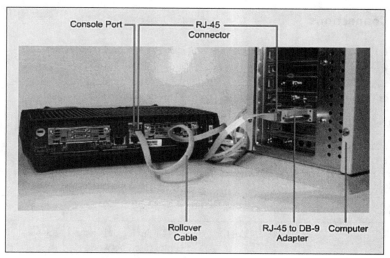

Terminal Settings

Figure 1-2 illustrates the settings that you should configure to have your PC connect to the router or switch.

Figure 1-2   *PC Settings to Connect to a Router or Switch*

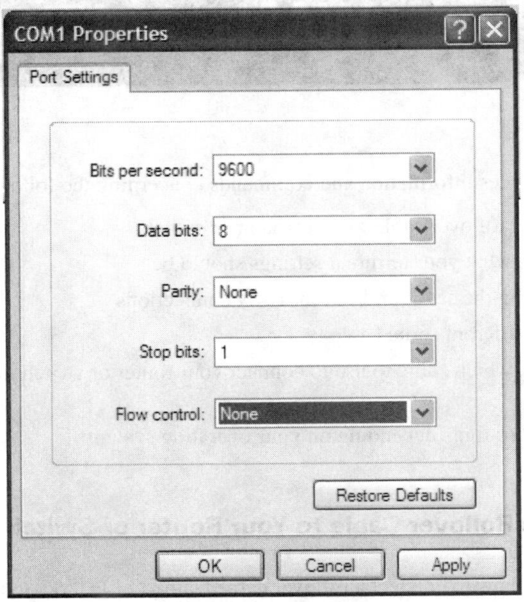

LAN Connections

Table 1-1 shows the various port types and connections between LAN devices.

Table 1-1   LAN Connections

Port or Connection	Port Type	Connected To	Cable
Ethernet	RJ-45	Ethernet hub or Ethernet switch	RJ-45
T1/E1 WAN	RJ-48C/CA81A	T1 or E1 network	Rollover
Console	8 pin	Computer COM port	Rollover
AUX	8 pin	Modem	RJ-45
BRI S/T	RJ-48C/CA81A	NT1 device or private integrated network exchange (PINX)	RJ-45
BRI U WAN	RJ-49C/CA11A	ISDN network	RJ-45

Serial Cable Types

Figure 1-3 shows the DB-60 end of a Serial cable that connects to a 2500 series router.

Figure 1-4 shows the newer smart serial end of a serial cable that connects to a smart serial port on your router.

Figure 1-5 shows examples of the male data terminal equipment (DTE) and the female data communications equipment (DCE) ends that are on the other side of a serial or smart serial cable.

Laptops released in the past few years come equipped with USB ports, not serial ports. For these newer laptops, you need a USB-to-serial connector, as illustrated in Figure 1-6.

Figure 1-3   Serial Cable (2500)

Figure 1-4   Smart Serial Cable (1700 or 2600)

Figure 1-5   *V.35 DTE and DCE Cables*

NOTE: CCNA focuses on *V.35 cables* for back-to-back connections between routers.

Figure 1-6   *USB-to-Serial Connector for Laptops*

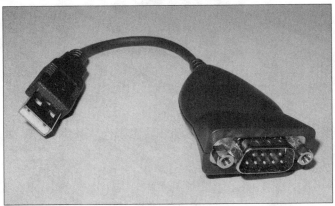

Which Cable to Use?

Table 1-2 describes which cable should be used when wiring your devices together. It is important to ensure you have proper cabling; otherwise, you might be giving yourself problems before you even get started.

Table 1-2   Determining Which Cables to Use When Wiring Devices Together

If device A has a:	And device B has a:	Then use this cable:
Computer COM port	Console of router/switch	Rollover
Computer NIC	Switch/hub	Straight-through
Computer NIC	Computer NIC	Crossover
Switch or hub port	Router's Ethernet port	Straight-through
Switch or hub port	Switch or hub port	Crossover (check for uplink button or toggle switch to defeat this)
Router's Ethernet port	Router's Ethernet port	Crossover
Computer NIC	Router's Ethernet port	Crossover
Router's serial port	Router's serial port	Cisco serial DCE/DTE cables

Table 1-3 lists the pinouts for straight-through, crossover, and rollover cables.

Table 1-3   Pinouts for Different Cables

Straight-Through Cable	Crossover Cable	Rollover Cable
Pin 1 – Pin 1	Pin 1 – Pin 3	Pin 1 – Pin 8
Pin 2 – Pin 2	Pin 2 – Pin 6	Pin 2 – Pin 7
Pin 3 – Pin 3	Pin 3 – Pin 1	Pin 3 – Pin 6
Pin 4 – Pin 4	Pin 4 – Pin 4	Pin 4 – Pin 5
Pin 5 – Pin 5	Pin 5 – Pin 5	Pin 5 – Pin 4
Pin 6 – Pin 6	Pin 6 – Pin 2	Pin 6 – Pin 3
Pin 7 – Pin 7	Pin 7 – Pin 7	Pin 7 – Pin 2
Pin 8 – Pin 8	Pin 8 – Pin 8	Pin 8 – Pin 1

OS IP Verification Commands

The following are commands that you should use to verify what your IP settings are. Different operating systems have different commands.

- **ipconfig** (Windows 2000/XP):

  Click **Start > Run > Command > ipconfig** or **ipconfig/all**.

- **winipcfg** (Windows 95/98/Me):

  Click **Start > Run > winipcfg**.

- **ifconfig** (Mac/Linux):

  `#ifconfig`

CHAPTER 2

Introduction to Routers

This chapter provides information and commands concerning the following topics:

- Navigating through command syntax and command modes
- The setup mode
- Keyboard help
- History commands
- **show** commands relating to these topics

Shortcuts for Entering Commands

To enhance efficiency, Cisco IOS Software has some shortcuts for entering commands. Although these are great to use in the real world, when it comes time to write a vendor exam, make sure you know the full commands, and not just the shortcuts.

Router>**enable** = Router>**enab** = Router>**en**	Entering a shortened form of a command is sufficient as long as there is no confusion over which command you are asking for
Router#**configure terminal** is the same as: Router#**config t**	

Using the (Tab⇆) Key to Complete Commands

Router#**sh** (Tab⇆) = Router#**show**	

Using the Question Mark for Help

The following output shows you how using the question mark can help you to work your way through a command and all of its parameters.

`Router#?`	Lists all commands available in the current command mode
`Router#c?` `clear  clock`	Lists all the possible choices that start with **c**
`Router#cl?` `clear    clock`	Lists all the possible choices that start with **cl**
`Router#clock`	
`% Incomplete Command`	Tells you that there are more parameters that need to be entered
`Router#clock ?` `set`	Shows all subcommands for this command Sets the time and date
`Router#clock set 19:50:00 14` `July 2003 ? `⏎Enter	Pressing the ⏎Enter key confirms the time and date configured
`Router#`	No Error message/Incomplete Command message means the command was entered successfully

enable Command

`Router>enable` `Router#`	Moves user from user mode to privileged mode

exit Command

`Router#exit   or` `Router>exit`	Logs a user off

`Router(config-`
`if)#exit`
`Router(config)#`
	Moves you back one level

`Router(config)#exit` `Router#`	Moves you back one level

disable Command

Router#disable Router>	Moves you from privileged mode back to user mode

logout Command

Router#logout	Performs the same function as **exit**

Setup Mode

Starts automatically if no startup configuration present.

Router#setup	Enters startup mode from the command line

NOTE: The answer inside the square brackets [ ] is the default answer. If this is the answer you want, just press ⏎Enter.

Pressing Ctrl c at any time will end the setup process, shut down all interfaces, and take you to user mode (**Router>**).

NOTE: Setup mode *cannot* be used to configure an entire router. It does only the basics. For example, you can only turn on either RIPv1 or IGRP, but not OSPF or EIGRP. You cannot create ACLs here or enable NAT. You can assign an IP address to an interface, but not a subinterface. All in all, setup mode is very limiting.

Entering setup mode is not a recommended practice. Instead, you should use the command-line interface (CLI), which is more powerful:

```
Would you like to enter the initial configuration dialog? [yes] : no
Would you like to enable autoinstall? [yes]   no
```

Autoinstall is a feature that will try and broadcast out all interfaces to try and find a configuration. If you say **yes**, you will have to wait for a few minutes while it looks for a configuration to load. Very frustrating. Say **no**.

Keyboard Help

The keystrokes described in Table 2-1 are meant to help you in your editing of the configuration. Because there are certain tasks that you want to do over and over again, Cisco IOS Software has in place certain keystroke combinations to help make the process more efficient.

Table 2-1 Keyboard Help

^ (carat symbol; above the 6 key) See next row for an example	Shows you where you made a mistake in entering a command
Router#**confog t** ^ % Invalid input detected at '^' marker. Router#**config t** Router(config)#	
Ctrl a	Moves cursor to beginning of line
Esc b	Moves cursor back one word
Ctrl b (or ← left arrow)	Moves cursor back one character
Ctrl e	Moves cursor to end of line
Ctrl f (or → right arrow)	Moves cursor forward one character
Esc f	Moves cursor forward one word
Ctrl z	Moves you from any prompt back down to privileged mode
$	Indicates that the line has been scrolled to the left
Router#**terminal no editing** Router#	Turns off the ability to use the previous keyboard shortcuts
Router#**terminal editing** Router#	Re-enables enhanced editing mode (can use above keyboard shortcuts)

History Commands

Ctrl p or ↑ (up arrow)	Recalls commands in the history buffer in a backward sequence, beginning with the most recent command
Ctrl n or ↓ (down arrow)	Returns to more recent commands in the history buffer after recalling commands with Ctrl P key sequence

`terminal history size` *number* See the next row for an example	Sets the number of commands in the buffer that can recalled by the router (maximum number is 256)
`Router#terminal history size 25`	Router will now remember the last 25 commands in the buffer
`Router#no terminal history size 25`	Sets history buffer back to 10 commands, which is the default

NOTE: The **history size** command provides the same function as the **terminal history size** command.

Be careful when you set the size to something larger than the default. By telling the router to keep the last 256 commands in a buffer, you are taking memory away from other parts of the router. What would you rather have: a router that remembers what you last typed in, or a router that routes as efficiently as possible?

show Commands

`Router#show version`	Displays information about current IOS
`Router#show flash`	Displays information about Flash memory
`Router#show history`	Lists all commands in the history buffer

NOTE: The last line of output from the **show version** command tells you what the configuration register is set to.

Configuring a Router

PART II CCNA 2

This chapter provides information and commands concerning the following topics:

- Configuring a router, specifically:
  - Names
  - Passwords
  - Interfaces
  - MOTD banners
  - IP host tables
  - Saving and erasing your configurations
- **show** commands to verify the router configurations

Router Modes

`Router>`	User mode
`Router#`	Privileged mode
`Router(config)#`	Global configuration mode
`Router(config-if)#`	Interface mode
`Router(config-subif)#`	Subinterface mode
`Router(config-line)#`	Line mode
`Router(config-router)#`	Router configuration mode

TIP: There are other modes than these. Not all commands work in all modes. Be careful. If you type in a command that you know is correct—**show run**, for example—and you get an error, make sure that you are in the correct mode.

Global Configuration Mode

`Router>`	Can see config, but not change
`Router#`	Can see config and move to make changes
`Router#config t` `Router(config)#`	Moves to global config mode This prompt indicates that you can start making changes

Configuring a Router Name

This command works on both routers and switches.

`Router(config)#hostname Cisco`
 	
`Cisco(config)#`
	Name can be any word you choose

Configuring Passwords

Works on both routers and switches.

`Router(config)#enable password cisco`	Sets enable password
`Router(config)#enable secret class`	Sets enable secret password
`Router(config)#line con 0`	Enters console-line mode
`Router(config-line)#password console`	Sets console-line mode password to **console**
`Router(config-line)#login`	Enables password checking at login
`Router(config)#line vty 0 4`	Enters vty line mode for all 5 vty lines
`Router(config-line)#password telnet`	Sets vty password to **telnet**
`Router(config-line)#login`	Enables password checking at login

Router(config)#**line aux 0**	Enters auxiliary line mode
Router(config-line)#**password** backdoor	Sets auxiliary line mode password to **backdoor**
Router(config-line)#**login**	Enables password checking at login

CAUTION: Enable secret password is encrypted by default. Enable password is not. For this reason, recommended practice is that you *never* use the enable password. Use only the enable secret password in a router configuration.

CAUTION: You cannot set both enable secret and enable password to the same password. Doing so defeats the use of encryption.

Password Encryption

Router(config)#**service password-encryption**	Applies a weak encryption to passwords
Router(config)#**enable password cisco**	Sets enable password to **cisco**
Router(config)#**line con 0**	...
Router(config-line)#**password Cisco**	Continue setting passwords as above
	...
Router(config)#**no service password-encryption**	Turns off password encryption

CAUTION: If you have turned on service password encryption, used it, and then turned it off, any passwords that you have encrypted will stay encrypted. New passwords will remain unencrypted

show Commands

Router#**show ?**	Lists all **show** commands available
Router#**show interfaces**	Displays statistics for all interfaces
Router#**show interface serial 0**	Displays statistics for a specific interface, in this case Serial 0
Router#**show ip interface brief**	Displays a summary of all interfaces, including status and IP address assigned

Router#**show controllers serial 0**	Displays statistics for interface hardware. Statistics display if the clock rate is set and if the cable is DCE, DTE, or not attached
Router#**show clock**	Displays time set on device
Router#**show hosts**	Displays local host-to-IP address cache. These are the names and addresses of hosts on the network to which you can connect
Router#**show users**	Displays all users connected to device
Router#**show history**	Displays history of commands used
Router#**show flash**	Displays info about Flash memory
Router#**show version**	Displays info about loaded software version
Router#**show arp**	Displays the ARP table
Router#**show protocols**	Displays status of configured Layer 3 protocols
Router#**show startup-config**	Displays configuration saved in NVRAM
Router#**show running-config**	Displays configuration currently running in RAM

Interface Names

One of the biggest problems that new administrators face is the names of the interfaces on the different models of routers. The following chart lists the names of the Ethernet, Fast Ethernet, and Serial interfaces on the 2500, 1700, and 2600 series of routers.

Fixed Interfaces (2500 Series)	Modular (Removable) Interfaces (1700 Series)	Modular (Removable) Interfaces (2600 Series)
Router(config)#**int erface** *type port*	Router(config)#**interf ace** *type port*	Router(config)#**interface** *type slot/port*
Router(config)#**int serial0 (s0)**	Router(config)#**interf ace serial 0**	Router(config)#**int serial 0/0 (s0/0)**
Router(config)#**int ethernet 0 (e0)**	Router(config)#**interf ace fastethernet 0**	Router(config)#**int fastethernet 0/0 (fa0/0)**

Moving Between Interfaces

What happens in Column 1 is the same thing as is occurring in Column 2.

`Router(config)#int s0`	`Router(config)#int s0`	Moves to interface S0 mode
`Router(config-if)#exit`	`Router(config-if)#int e0`	In int S0, move to E0
`Router(config)#int e0`	`Router(config-if)#`	In E0 mode now
`Router(config-if)#`		Prompt does not change; be *careful*

Configuring a Serial Interface

`Router(config)#int s0/0`	Moves to interface Serial 0/0 mode
`Router(config-if)#description Link to ISP`	Optional descriptor of the link is locally significant
`Router(config-if)#ip address 192.168.10.1 255.255.255.0`	Assigns address and subnet mask to interface
`Router(config-if)#clock rate 56000`	Assigns a clock rate for the interface
`Router(config-if)#no shut`	Turns interface on

TIP: The **clock rate** command is used *only* on a *serial* interface that has a *DCE* cable plugged into it. There must be a clock rate set on every serial link between routers. It does not matter which router has the DCE cable plugged into it, or which interface the cable is plugged into. Serial 0 on one router can be plugged into Serial 1 on another router.

Configuring an Ethernet/Fast Ethernet Interface

`Router(config)#int fa0/0`	Moves to Fast Ethernet 0/0 interface mode
`Router(config-if)#description Accounting LAN`	Optional descriptor of the link is locally significant

Router(config-if)#ip address 192.168.20.1 255.255.255.0	Assigns address and subnet mask to interface
Router(config-if)#no shut	Turns interface on

Creating a MOTD Banner

Router(config)#banner motd # This is a secure system. Authorized Personnel Only! # Router(config)#	# is known as a *delimiting character*. The delimiting character must surround the banner message and can be any character so long as it is not a character used within the body of the message

Setting the Clock Time Zone

Router(config)#clock timezone EST -5	Sets the time zone for display purposes. Based on coordinated universal time (Eastern Standard Time is 5 hours behind UTC)

Assigning a Local Host Name to an IP Address

Router(config)#ip host london 172.16.1.3	Assigns a host name to the IP address. After this assignment, you can use the host name instead of an IP address when trying to Telnet or ping to that address
Router#ping london = Router#ping 172.16.1.3	

TIP: The default port number in the **ip host** command is 23, or Telnet. If you want to Telnet to a device, just enter the IP host name itself:

Router#london = Router#telnet london = Router#telnet 172.16.1.3

no ip domain-lookup Command

Router(config)#`no ip domain-lookup` Router(config)#	Turns off trying to automatically resolve an unrecognized command to a local host name

TIP: Ever type in a command incorrectly and left having to wait for a minute or two as the router tries to *translate* your command to a domain server of 255.255.255.255? The router is set by default to try to resolve any word that is not a command to a DNS server at address 255.255.255.255. If you are not going to set up DNS, turn this feature off to save you time as you type, especially if you are a poor typist.

logging synchronous Command

Router(config)#`line con 0`	
Router(config-line)#`logging synchronous`	Turns on synchronous logging. Information items sent to console will not interrupt the command you are typing. The command will be moved to a new line

TIP: Ever try to type in a command and an informational line appears in the middle of what you were typing? Lose your place? Do not know where you are in the command, so you just press ⏎Enter and start all over? The **logging synchronous** command will tell the router that if any informational items get displayed on the screen, your prompt and command line should be moved to a new line, so as not to confuse you.

The informational line does not get inserted into the middle of the command you are trying to type. If you were to continue typing, the command would execute properly, even though it looks wrong on the screen

exec-timeout Command

Router(config)#`line con 0`	
Router(config-line)#`exec-timeout 0 0`	Sets time limit when console automatically logs off. Set to **0 0** (minutes seconds) means console never logs off
Router(config-line)#	

TIP: **exec-timeout 0 0** is great for a lab because the console never logs out. This is very dangerous in the real world (bad security).

Saving Configurations

`Router#copy run start`	Saves the running-config to local NVRAM
`Router#copy run tftp`	Saves the running-config remotely to TFTP server

Erasing Configurations

`Router#erase start`	Deletes the startup-config file from NVRAM

TIP: Running-config is still in dynamic memory. Reload the router to clear the running-config.

Configuration Example: Basic Router Configuration

Figure 3-1 shows the network topology for the configuration that follows, which shows a basic router configuration using the commands covered in this chapter.

Figure 3-1   Network Topology for Basic Router Configuration

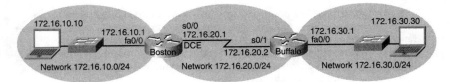

Boston Router

`Router>en`	Enters privileged mode
`Router#clock set 18:30:00 15 Nov 2004`	Sets local time on router
`Router#config t`	Enters global config mode

`Router(config)#hostname Boston`	Sets router name to **Boston**
`Boston(config)#no ip domain-lookup`	Turns off name resolution on unrecog-nized commands (spelling mistakes)

`Boston(config)#banner motd #`
`This is  the Boston Router.`
`Authorized Access Only`
`#`
	Creates an MOTD banner

`Boston(config)#clock timezone EST -5`	Sets time zone to Eastern Standard Time (–5 from UTC)
`Boston(config)#enable secret cisco`	Enable secret password set to **cisco**
`Boston(config)#service password-encryption`	Passwords will be given weak encryption
`Boston(config)#line con 0`	Enters line console mode
`Boston(config-line)#logging sync`	Commands will not be interrupted by unsolicited messages
`Boston(config-line)#password class`	Sets password to **class**
`Boston(config-line)#login`	Enables password checking at login
`Boston(config-line)#line vty 0 4`	Moves to virtual Telnet lines 0 through 4
`Boston(config-line)#password class`	Sets password to **class**
`Boston(config-line)#login`	Enables password checking at login
`Boston(config-line)#line aux 0`	Moves to line auxiliary mode
`Boston(config-line)#password class`	Sets password to **class**
`Boston(config-line)#login`	Enables password checking at login
`Boston(config-line)#exit`	Moves back to global config mode

Boston(config)#no service password-encryption	Turns off password encryption
Boston(config)#int fa 0/0	Moves to Fast Ethernet 0/0 mode
Boston(config-if)#desc Engineering LAN	Sets locally significant description of the interface
Boston(config-if)#ip address 172.16.10.1 255.255.255.0	Assigns IP address and subnet mask to the interface
Boston(config-if)#no shut	Turns on the interface
Boston(config-if)#int s0/0	Moves directly to Serial 0/0 mode
Boston(config-if)#desc Link to Buffalo Router	Sets locally significant description of the interface
Boston(config-if)#ip address 172.16.20.1 255.255.255.0	Assigns IP address and subnet mask to the interface
Boston(config-if)#clock rate 56000	Sets a clock rate for serial transmission (DCE cable must be plugged into this interface)
Boston(config-if)#no shut	Turns on the interface
Boston(config-if)#exit	Moves back to global config mode
Boston(config)#ip host buffalo 172.16.20.2	Sets a local host name resolution to IP address 172.16.20.2
Boston(config)#exit	Moves back to privileged mode
Boston#copy run start	Saves running-config to NVRAM

CHAPTER 4

Learning About Other Devices

This chapter provides information and commands concerning the following topics:

- Commands related to Cisco Discovery Protocol (CDP)
- Using Telnet to remotely connect to other devices

Cisco Discovery Protocol

Router#**show cdp**	Displays global CDP information (such as timers)
Router#**show cdp neighbors**	Displays information about neighbors
Router#**show cdp neighbors detail**	Displays more detail about neighbor device
Router#**show cdp entry word**	Displays information about device named word
Router#**show cdp entry ***	Displays information about all devices
Router#**show cdp interface**	Displays info about interfaces that have CDP running
Router#**show cdp interface** *x*	Displays info about specific interface *x* running CDP
Router#**show cdp traffic**	Displays traffic info—packets in/out/version
Router(config)#**cdp holdtime** *x*	Changes length of time to keep CDP packets
Router(config)#**cdp timer** *x*	Changes how often CDP updates are sent
Router(config)#**cdp run**	Enables CDP globally (on by default)
Router(config)#**no cdp run**	Turns off CDP globally

`Router(config-if)#cdp enable`	Enables CDP on a specific interface
`Router(config-if)#no cdp enable`	Turns off CDP on a specific interface
`Router#clear cdp counters`	Resets traffic counters to 0
`Router#clear cdp table`	Deletes the CDP table
`Router#debug cdp adjacency`	Monitors CDP neighbor information
`Router#debug cdp events`	Monitors all CDP events
`Router#debug cdp ip`	Monitors CDP events specifically for IP
`Router#debug cdp packets`	Monitors CDP packet-related information

CAUTION: Although CDP is an excellent source of information to you the network administrator, is it a potential security risk if a hacker gains access to one of your systems. The information that you gain through CDP is also gained by the hacker.

After you have used CDP to gather your information in a production environment, turn it off to thwart any bad people from using it for no good.

Telnet

The following five commands all achieve the same result—the attempt to connect remotely to the router named paris at IP address 172.16.20.1.

`Denver>telnet paris`	Enter if **ip host** command was used previously to create a mapping of an IP address to the word paris
`Denver>telnet 172.16.20.1`	
`Denver>paris`	Enter if **ip host** command is using default port #
`Denver>connect paris`	
`Denver>172.16.20.1`	

Any of the preceding commands lead to the following configuration sequence:

`Paris>`	As long as vty password is set (See caution following this table)
`Paris>`**`exit`**	Terminates the Telnet session
`Denver>`	
`Paris>`**`logout`**	Terminates the Telnet session
`Denver>`	
`Paris>`⌨Ctrl⌨⇧Shift⌨6, `release, then press` ⌨x	Suspends the Telnet session, but does not terminate it
`Denver>`	
`Denver>`⌨↵Enter	Resumes the connection to paris
`Paris>`	
`Denver>`**`resume`**	Resumes the connection to paris
`Paris>`	
`Denver>`**`disconnect paris`**	Terminates the session to paris
`Denver>`	
`Denver#`**`show sessions`**	Displays connections you opened to other sites
`Denver#`**`show users`**	Displays who is connected remotely to you

`Denver#`**`clear line`** `x`	Disconnects remote user connected to you on line *x* Line number is listed in the output gained from the **show users** command
`Denver(config)#`**`line vty 0 4`**	
`Denver(config-line)` **`session-limit`** `x`	Limits the number of simultaneous sessions per vty line to *x* amount

CAUTION: The following configuration creates a big security hole. Never use in a live production environment. Use in the lab only!

`Denver(config)#`**`line vty 0 4`**	.
`Denver(config-line)#`**`no password`**	Remote user is not challenged when Telnetting to this device
`Denver(config-line)#`**`no login`**	Remote user moves straight to user mode

NOTE: A device must have two passwords for a remote user to be able to make changes to your configuration:

- Line vty password (or have it explicitly turned off; see previous Caution)
- Enable or enable secret password

Without the enable or enable secret password, a remote user will only be able to get to user mode, not to privileged mode. This is extra security.

ping

`Router#`**`ping 172.168.20.1`**	Performs basic Layer 3 test to address
`Router#`**`ping paris`**	Same as above but through IP host name
`Router#`**`ping`**	Enters extended ping mode. Can now change parameters of ping test

`Protocol [ip]:` ⏎Enter	Press ⏎Enter to use ping for IP
`Target IP address: `**172.16.20.1**	Enter target IP address
`Repeat count [5]:`**100**	Enter number of echo requests you want to send. 5 is the default
`Datagram size [100]:`⏎Enter	Enter size of datagrams being sent. 100 is the default
`Timeout in Seconds [2]:`⏎Enter	Enter timeout delay between sending echo requests
`Extended commands [n]: `**yes**	Allows you to configure extended commands
`Source address or interface: `**10.0.10.1**	Allows you to explicitly set where the pings are originating from
`Type of Service [0]`	Allows you to set the TOS field in the IP Header
`Set DF bit in IP header [no]`	Allows you to set the DF bit in the IP Header
`Validate reply data? [no]`	Allows you to set whether you want validation
`Data Pattern [0xABCD]`	Allows you to change the data pattern in the data field of the ICMP Echo request packet

`Loose, Strict, Record, Timestamp, Verbose[none]:`⏎Enter
 	
`Sweep range of sizes [no]: `⏎Enter
 	
`Type escape sequence to abort`
 	
`Sending 100, 100-byte ICMP Echos to 172.16.20.1, timeout is 2 seconds:`
 	
`!!!!!!!!!!!!!!!!!!!!!!!!!!!!!!!!!!!!!!!!!!!!!!!!!!!`
`!!!!!!!!!!!!!!!!!!!!!!!!!!!!!!!!!!!!!!!!!!!!!!!!!!!`
`!!!!!!!!!!!!!!!!!!!!!!!!!!!!!!!!!!!!`
 	
`Success rate is 100 percent (100/100) round-trip min/avg/max = 1/1/4 ms`	

traceroute

`Router#traceroute 172.168.20.1`	Discovers route taken to travel to destination
`Router#trace paris`	Short form of command with IP host name

CHAPTER 5

Managing Cisco IOS Software

This chapter provides information and commands concerning the following topics:

- Changing the order of from where IOS is loaded
- The configuration register
- Pre-IOS 12.0 commands versus 12.x commands
- Backing up and restoring configurations and IOS using TFTP
- Restoring IOS using Xmodem
- Restoring IOS using **tftpdnld**
- Password recovery procedures

Boot System Commands

Router(config)#**boot system flash** *image-name*	Loads IOS with *image-name*
Router(config)#**boot system tftp** *image-name* **172.16.10.3**	Loads IOS with *image-name* from a TFTP server
Router(config)#**boot system rom**	Loads IOS from ROM
Router(config)#**exit**	
Router#**copy run start**	Saves running-configuration to NVRAM Router will execute commands in order they were entered on next reload

If you enter **boot system flash** first, that is the first place the router will go to look for the IOS. If you want to go to a TFTP server first, make sure that the **boot system tftp** command is the first one you enter.

Configuration Register

Router#**show version**	Last line tells you what the configuration register is set to
Router#**config t** Router(config)#**config-register 0x2142**	Changes the configuration register setting to 2142

Cisco IOS Software Prerelease 12.0 Commands Versus Cisco IOS Software 12.x Commands

Pre-IOS 12.0 Commands	IOS 12.x Commands
copy tftp running-config	**copy tftp: system:running-config**
copy tftp startup-config	**copy tftp: nvram:startup-config**
show startup-config	**more nvram:startup-config**
erase startup-config	**erase nvram:**
copy run start	**copy system:running-config nvram:startup-config**
copy run tftp	**copy system:running-config tftp:**
show run	**more system:running-config**

Backing Up Configurations

Denver#**copy run start**	Saves running-config from DRAM to NVRAM (locally)
Denver#**copy run tftp**	Copies running-config to remote TFTP server
Address or name of remote host[ ]? **192.168.119.20**	IP address of TFTP server
Destination Filename [Denver-confg]?⏎Enter	Name to use for file saved on TFTP server
!!!!!!!!!!!!!!!!	Each bang symbol (!) = 1 datagram of data
624 bytes copied in 7.05 secs	
Denver#	File has been transferred successfully

NOTE: You can also use the preceding sequence for a **copy start tftp** command sequence.

Restoring Configurations

`Denver#`**`copy tftp run`**	Copies configuration file from TFTP server to DRAM
`    Address or name of remote host[ ]?` **`192.168.119.20`**	IP address of TFTP server
`    Source filename [ ]?`**`Denver-confg`**	Enter the name of the file you want to retrieve
`    Destination filename [running-config]?`(⏎`Enter`)	
`    Accessing tftp://192.168.119.20/Denver-confg…`	
`    Loading Denver-confg from 192.168.119.02 (via Fast Ethernet 0/0):`	
`    !!!!!!!!!!!!!!!!`	
`    [OK-624 bytes]`	
`    624 bytes copied in 9.45 secs`	
`Denver#`	File has been transferred successfully

NOTE: You can also use the preceding sequence for a **copy tftp start** command sequence.

Backing Up IOS to a TFTP Server

`Denver#`**`copy flash tftp`**	
`    Source filename [ ]?` **`c2600-js-l_121-3.bin`**	Name of IOS image
`    Address or name of remote host [ ]?` **`192.168.119.20`**	Address of TFTP server
`    Destination filename [c2600-js-l_121-3.bin]?`(⏎`Enter`)	Destination filename is the same as the source filename, so just press (⏎`Enter`)

`!!!!!!!!!!!!!!!!!!!!!!!!!!!!!!!!!!!!!!!!!!!!!!!!!` `!!!!!!!!!!!!!!!!!!!!!!!!!!!!!!!!!!!!!!!!!`	
`8906589 bytes copied in 263.68 seconds`	
`Denver#`	

Restoring/Upgrading IOS from a TFTP Server

`Denver#`**`copy tftp flash`**	
`Address or name of remote host [ ]?` **`192.168.119.20`**	
`Source filename [ ]?` **`c2600-js-l_121-3.bin`**	
`Destination filename [c2600-js-l_121-` `3.bin]?`⏎Enter	
`Accessing tftp://192.168.119.20/c2600-js-` `l_121-3.bin`	
`Erase flash: before copying?` `[confirm]`⏎Enter	If Flash memory is full, must erase it first
`Erasing the flash file system will remove` `all files`	
`Continue? [confirm]`⏎Enter	Press Ctrl C if you want to cancel
`Erasing device   eeeeeeeeeeeeeeeeeee...erased`	Each "e" represents data being erased
`Loading c2600-js-l_121-3.bin from` `192.168.119.20`	
`(via) FastEthernet 0/0):` `!!!!!!!!!!!!!!!!!!!!!!!!!!!!!!!!!!!!!!!!!!!!!!!!!` `!!!!!!!!!!!!!!!!!!!!!!!!!!!!!!!!!!!!!!!!!!!!!!!!!` `!!!`	Each bang symbol (!) = 1 datagram of data
`Verifying Check sum ............... OK`	
`[OK - 8906589 Bytes]`	
`8906589 bytes copied in 277.45 secs`	
`Denver#`	Success

Restoring IOS from ROMmon Mode Using Xmodem

The output that follows was taken from a 1720 router. Some of this output might vary from yours, depending on the router model that you are using.

```rommon 1 >confreg```	Shows configuration summary. Step through the questions, answering defaults until you can change the console baud rate. Change it to 115200; makes transfer go faster

```   Configuration Summary```
```enabled are:```
```load rom after netboot fails```
```console baud: 9600```
```boot: image specified by the boot system commands```
``` or default to: cisco2-c1700```	

```do you wish to change the configuration? y/n [n]: y```
```enable   "diagnostic mode"? y/n [n]: n```
```enable   "use net in IP bcast address"? y/n [n]: n```
```disable   "load rom after netboot fails"? y/n [n]: n```
```enable   "use all zero broadcast"? y/n [n]: n```
```enable   "break/abort has effect"? y/n [n]: n```
```enable   "ignore system config info"? y/n [n]: n```
```change console baud rate? y/n [n]: y```
```enter rate: 0=9600, 1=4800, 2=1200, 3=2400```
```   4=19200, 5=38400, 6=57600, 7=115200 [0]: 7```
```change the boot characteristics? y/n [n]: n```
	Prompts will begin to ask a series of questions that will allow you to change the config-register. Answer **n** to all questions except the one that asks you to change the console baud rate. For the enter rate, choose **7** because that is the number that represents a baud rate of 115200

``
          Configuration Summary
enabled are:
load rom after netboot fails
console baud: 115200
boot: image specified by the boot
system commands
          or default to: cisco2-c1700
do you wish to change the
configuration? y/n [n]: n
 	
rommon2>
``
	After the summary is shown again, choose **n** to not change the configuration and go to the **rommon>** prompt again

``` rommon 2>reset ```	Reloads router at new com speed. Change HyperTerminal setting to 115200 to match the router's new console setting
``` Rommon 1>xmodem c1700-js-l_121-3.bin ```	Asking to transfer this image using Xmodem
`...<output cut>...`	
`Do you wish to continue? y/n [n ]:y`	Choose **y** to continue
	In HyperTerminal, go to Transfer, then Send File (see Figure 5-1). Locate the IOS file on the hard drive and click Send (see Figure 5-2)
``` Router will reload when transfer is completed ```	
`Reset baud rate on router`	

`Router(config)#`**`line con 0`**	
`Router(config-line)#`**`speed 9600`**	
`Router(config-line)#`**`exit`**	HyperTerminal will stop responding. Reconnect to the router using 9600 baud, 8-N-1

Figure 5-1   Finding the IOS Image File

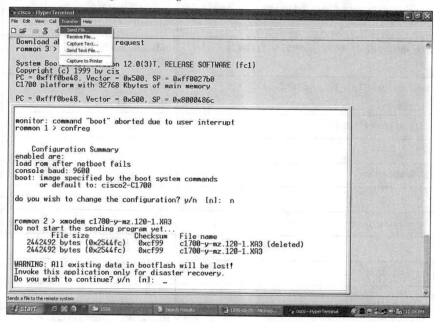

Figure 5-2   Sending the IOS Image File to the Router

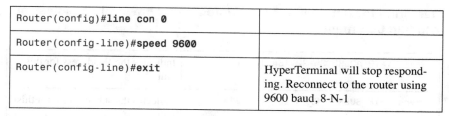

Restoring the IOS Using the ROMmon Environmental Variables and tftpdnld Command

`rommon 1>IP_ADDRESS=192.168.100.1`	Indicates the IP address for this unit
`rommon 2>IP_SUBNET_MASK=255.255.255.0`	Indicates the subnet mask for this unit
`rommon 3>DEFAULT_GATEWAY=192.168.100.1`	Indicates the default gateway for this unit
`rommon 4>TFTP_SERVER=192.168.100.2`	Indicates the IP address of the TFTP server
`rommon 5>TFTP_FILE= c2600-js-l_121-3.bin`	Indicates the filename to fetch from the TFTP server
`rommon 6>tftpdnld`	Starts the process
`…<output cut>…`	
`Do you wish to continue? y/n:  [n]:y`	
`…<output cut>…`	
`Rommon 7>i`	Resets the router (**i** stands for initialize)

NOTE: Commands and environmental variables are case sensitive, so be sure that you have not accidentally added spaces between variables and answers.

Password Recovery Procedures

Step	2500 Series Commands	1700/2600 Series Commands
Step 1: Boot the router and interrupt the boot sequence as soon as text appears on the screen.	Press Ctrl Break >	Press Ctrl Break rommon 1>
Step 2: Change the configuration register to ignore contents of NVRAM.	>o/r 0x2142	rommon 1>confreg 0x2142
	>	rommon 2>
Step 3: Reload the router.	>i	rommon 2>reset
Step 4: Enter privileged mode (do not enter setup mode).	Router>en	Router>en
	Router#	Router#
Step 5: Copy startup-config into running-config.	Router#copy start run	Router#copy start run
	...<output cut>...	...<output cut>...
	Denver#	Denver#
Step 6: Change the password.	Denver#config t	Denver#config t
	Denver(config)#enable secret *new*	Denver(config)#enable secret *new*
	Denver(config)#	Denver(config)#
Step 7: Reset configuration-register back to default value.	Denver(config)#config-register 0x2102	Denver(config)#config-register 0x2102

	Denver(config)#	Denver(config)#
Step 8: Save the configuration.	Denver(config)#**exit**	Denver(config)#**exit**
	Denver#**copy run start**	Denver#**copy run start**
	Denver#	Denver#
Step 9: Verify configuration register.	Denver#**show version**	Denver#**show version**
	...<output cut>...	...<output cut>...
	Configuration register is 0x2142 (will be 0x2102 at next reload)	Configuration register is 0x2142 (will be 0x2102 at next reload)
	Denver#	Denver#
Step 10: Reload the router.	Denver#**reload**	Denver#**reload**

CHAPTER 6

Routing and Routing Protocols

This chapter provides information and commands concerning the following topics:

- Configuring a static route on a router
- Configuring a default route on a router
- Verifying static routes

Static Routing

When using the **ip route** command, you can identify where packets should be routed to in two ways:

- The next-hop address
- The exit interface

Both ways are shown in both the "Configuration Example: Static Routes" section and the "Default Routing" section.

`Router(config)#ip route 172.16.20.0 255.255.255.0 172.16.10.2`	172.16.20.0 = destination network 255.255.255.0 = subnet mask 172.16.10.2 = next-hop address Read this to say: To get to the destination network of 172.16.20.0, with a subnet mask of 255.255.255.0, send all packets to 172.16.10.2
`Router(config)#ip route 172.16.20.0 255.255.255.0 s0/0`	172.16.20.0 = destination network 255.255.255.0 = subnet mask s0/0 = exit interface Read this to say: To get to the destination network of 172.16.20.0, with a subnet mask of 255.255.255.0, send all packets out interface Serial 0/0

Default Routing

`Router(config)#ip route 0.0.0.0 0.0.0.0` `172.16.10.2`	Send all packets destined for networks not in my routing table to 172.16.10.2
`Router(config)#ip route 0.0.0.0 0.0.0.0 s0/0`	Send all packets destined for networks not in my routing table out my Serial 0/0 interface

Verifying Static Routes

`Router#show ip route`	Displays contents of IP routing table

NOTE: The codes to the left of the routes in the table tell you from where the router learned the routes. A static route is described by the letter S.

Configuration Example: Static Routes

Figure 6-1 shows the network topology for the configuration that follows, which shows how to configure static routes using the commands covered in this chapter.

Figure 6-1   Network Topology for Static Route Configuration

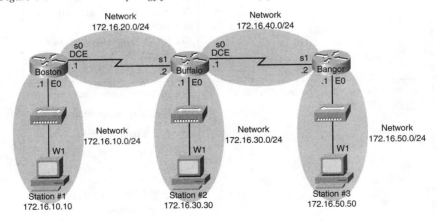

NOTE: The host name, password, and interfaces have all been configured as per the configuration in the Chapter 3 configuration example.

Boston Router

Boston>en	
Boston#config t	
Boston(config)#ip route 172.16.30.0 255.255.255.0 172.16.20.2	Configures a static route using the next-hop address
Boston(config)#ip route 172.16.40.0 255.255.255.0 172.16.20.2	
Boston(config)#ip route 172.16.50.0 255.255.255.0 172.16.20.2	
Boston(config)#exit	
Boston#copy run start	

Buffalo Router

Buffalo>en	
Buffalo#config t	
Buffalo(config)#ip route 172.16.10.0 255.255.255.0 s1	Configures a static route using the exit interface
Buffalo(config)#ip route 172.16.50.0 255.255.255.0 s0	
Boston(config)#exit	
Boston#copy run start	

Bangor Router

Bangor>en	
Bangor#config t	
Bangor(config)#ip route 0.0.0.0 0.0.0.0 s1	Configures a static route using the default route
Bangor(config)#exit	
Bangor#copy run start	

CHAPTER 7

Distance Vector Routing Protocols

This chapter provides information and commands concerning the following topics:

- Mandatory and optional commands for configuring the Routing Information Protocol (RIP)
- Commands for configuring the RIP Version 2 (RIP-2) routing protocol
- Mandatory and optional commands for configuring the Interior Gateway Routing Protocol (IGRP)
- Dynamic routing protocol options
- Troubleshooting dynamic routing protocols
- Verifying routing

IP Classless

`Router(config)#ip classless`	Instructs IOS to forward packets destined for an unknown subnet to the best supernet route
`Router(config)#no ip classless`	Turns off the **ip classless** command

NOTE: A supernet route is a route that covers a range of subnets with a single entry

NOTE: The **ip classless** command is enabled by default in Cisco IOS Software Release 11.3 and later.

RIP Routing: Mandatory Commands

`Router(config)#router rip`	Enables RIP as a routing protocol
`Router(config-router)#network w.x.y.z`	*w.x.y.z* is the network number of the *directly connected* network you want to advertise

NOTE: You need to advertise only the classful network number, not a subnet:

```
Router(config-router)#network 172.16.0.0
```

not

```
Router(config-router)#network 172.16.10.0
```

If you advertise a subnet, you will not receive an error message, because the router will automatically convert the subnet to the classful network address.

RIP Routing: Optional Commands

`Router(config)#no router rip`	Turns off the RIP routing process
`Router(config-router)#no network w.x.y.z`	Removes network *w.x.y.z* from the RIP routing process
`Router(config-router)#passive-interface s0/0`	RIP updates will not be sent out this interface
`Router(config-router)#neighbor a.b.c.d`	Defines a specific neighbor with which to exchange information
`Router(config-router)#no ip split-horizon`	Turns off split horizon (on by default)
`Router(config-router)#ip split-horizon`	Re-enables split horizon
`Router(config-router#timers basic 30 90 180 270 360`	Changes timers in RIP: 30 = Update timer (in seconds) 90 = Invalid timer (in seconds) 180 = Hold-down timer (in seconds) 270 = Flush timer (in seconds) 360 = Sleep time (in milliseconds)
`Router(config-router)#maximum-paths x`	Limits the number of paths for load balancing to *x* (4 = default, 6 = maximum)
`Router(config-router)#default-information originate`	Generates a default route into RIP

RIP Version 2

NOTE: RIP-2 is not part of the CCNA certification exam. Commands are listed here for reference only.

`Router(config-router)#version 2`	RIP will now send and receive RIP-2 packets globally
`Router(config-if)#ip rip send version 1`	Interface will send only RIP-1 packets
`Router(config-if)#ip rip send version 2`	Interface will send only RIP-2 packets
`Router(config-if)#ip rip send version 1 2`	Interface will send both RIP-1 and RIP-2 packets
`Router(config-if)#ip rip receive version 1`	Interface will receive only RIP-1 packets
`Router(config-if)#ip rip receive version 2`	Interface will receive only RIP-2 packets
`Router(config-if)#ip rip receive version 1 2`	Interface will receive both RIP-1 and RIP-2 packets

Troubleshooting RIP Issues

`Router#debug ip rip`	Displays all RIP activity in real time
`Router#show ip rip database`	Displays contents of the RIP database

IGRP Routing: Mandatory Commands

`Router(config)#router igrp` `as-number`	Enables IGRP routing process. The autono-mous system number (*as-number*) used in the IGRP routing process *must match* all other routers in order for communication to take place

`Router(config-router)#network w.x.y.z`	*w.x.y.z* is the network number of the *directly connected* network you want to advertise

NOTE: You need to advertise only the classful network number, not a subnet:

`Router(config-router)#network 172.16.0.0`

not

`Router(config-router)#network 172.16.10.0`

If you advertise a subnet, you will not receive an error message, because the router will automatically convert the subnet to the classful network address.

IGRP Routing: Optional Commands

`Router(config)#no router igrp as-number`	Disables the IGRP routing process
`Router(config-router)#no network w.x.y.z`	Removes network *w.x.y.z* from the IGRP routing process
`Router(config-if)#bandwidth x`	Sets the bandwidth of this interface to *x* kilobits to allow IGRP to make a better routing decision
`Router(config-router)#variance x`	Allows IGRP to accept unequal-cost routes

Troubleshooting IGRP Issues

`Router#debug ip igrp events`	Shows all IGRP events in real time
`Router#debug ip igrp transactions`	Shows IGRP updates between routers

CAUTION: IGRP as a routing protocol is no longer supported by Cisco as of Cisco IOS Software Release 12.3. If you are using Cisco IOS 12.3 or newer code, you must use either Enhanced IGRP (EIGRP) or one of the other standards—RIP-1, RIP-2, or OSPF.

Dynamic Routing Protocol Options

`Router(config-if)#ip route-cache`	Controls the use of high-speed switching caches for IP routing
`Router(config-if)#no ip route-cache`	Disables any set switching modes from previous command
`Router(config)#ip default-network` *w.x.y.z*	Selects a network as a route for generat-ing a gateway of last resort
`Router(config-router)#redistribute static`	Takes static routes and redistributes them into a dynamic routing process

Troubleshooting Dynamic Routing Protocol Issues

`Router#debug ip packet`	Displays information about *all* IP debugging information
`Router#undebug all`	Turns off *all* debugging

NOTE: Use the short form of **undebug all** to quickly turn off all debugging commands:

`Router#u all`

Verifying Routing

`Router#show ip route`	Displays the current routing table
`Router#clear ip route *`	Deletes the current routing table and forces a rebuild of the table
`Router#show ip protocols`	Displays the current state of all active routing protocol processes
`Router#show interfaces`	Displays statistics for all interfaces

`Router#show interface fa 0/0`	Displays statistics for interface fa0/0
`Router#show ip interfaces`	Displays IP statistics for all interfaces
`Router#show ip interface fa 0/0`	Displays IP statistics for interface fa0/0
`Router#show ip interfaces brief`	Displays a summary of all interfaces, their status, and configured IP addresses
`Router#show running-config`	Displays the running-config
`Router#show run ¦ begin word`	Displays the running-config beginning with first instance of *word*, which can be any string of characters—numbers or letters

Configuration Example: Dynamic Routing

Figure 7-1 shows the network topology for the configuration that follows, which shows a dynamic routing configuration using the commands covered in this chapter.

Figure 7-1   Network Topology for Dynamic Routing Configuration

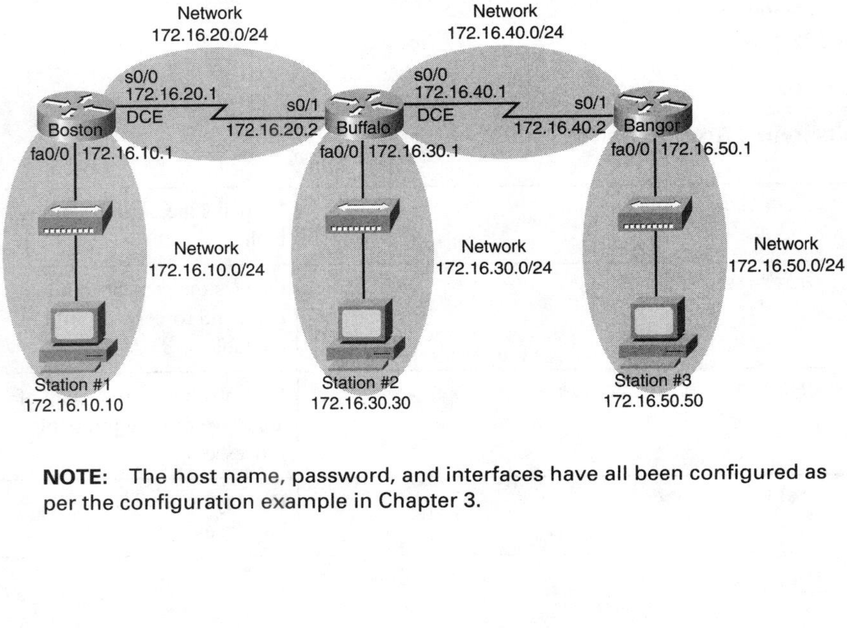

NOTE: The host name, password, and interfaces have all been configured as per the configuration example in Chapter 3.

Boston Router

Boston>en	
Boston#config t	
Boston(config)#no ip route 172.16.30.0 255.255.255.0 172.16.20.2	Removes static routes
Boston(config)#no ip route 172.16.40.0 255.255.255.0 172.16.20.2	
Boston(config)#no ip route 172.16.50.0 255.255.255.0 172.16.20.2	
Boston(config)#router rip or Boston(config)#router igrp 10	Enables RIP (or IGRP) routing IGRP routers *must* have the same autonomous system (AS) number
Boston(config-router)#network 172.16.0.0	Advertises directly connected networks (classful address only)
Boston(config-router)#exit	
Boston(config)#exit	
Boston#copy run start	

Buffalo Router

Buffalo>en	
Buffalo#config t	
Buffalo(config)#no ip route 172.16.10.0 255.255.255.0 s0/1	Removes static routes
Buffalo(config)#no ip route 172.16.50.0 255.255.255.0 s0/0	
Buffalo(config)#router rip or Buffalo(config)#router igrp 10	Enables RIP (or IGRP) routing IGRP routers have same the same AS number

`Buffalo(config-router)#network 172.16.0.0`	Advertises directly connected networks (classful address only)
`Buffalo(config-router)#`Ctrl z	Exits back to privileged mode
`Boston#copy run start`	

Bangor Router

`Bangor>en`	
`Bangor#config t`	
`Bangor(config)#no ip route 0.0.0.0 0.0.0.0 s0/1`	Removes static default route

`Bangor(config)#router rip`
or
`Bangor(config)#router igrp 10`
	Enables RIP (or IGRP) routing
	
	IGRP routers have the same AS number

`Bangor(config-router)#network 172.16.0.0`	Advertises directly connected networks (classful address only)
`Bangor(config-router)#`Ctrl z	Exits back to privileged mode
`Bangor#copy run start`	

CHAPTER 8

TCP/IP Suite Error and Control Messages

This chapter provides information and commands concerning the following topics:

- ICMP redirect messages
- The **ping** command

ICMP Redirect Messages

`Router(config-if)#no ip redirects`	Disables ICMP redirects from this specific interface
`Router(config-if)#ip redirects`	Re-enables ICMP redirects from this specific interface

ping Command

`Router#ping w.x.y.z`	Checks for Layer 3 connectivity with device at address *w.x.y.z*
`Router#ping`	Enters extended ping mode, which provides more options

TIP: See Part II, "CCNA 2," Chapter 4, "Learning About Other Devices," for output of an extended **ping** command.

The following table describes the possible **ping** output characters.

Character	Meaning
!	Successful receipt of a reply
.	Device timed out while waiting for reply
U	A destination unreachable error PDU was received

Q	Source quench (destination too busy)
M	Could not fragment
?	Unknown packet type
&	Packet lifetime exceeded

CHAPTER 9

Basic Router Troubleshooting

This chapter provides information and commands concerning the following topics:

- Viewing the routing table
- Determining the gateway of last resort
- Determining the last routing update
- Testing OSI Layers 3 and 7
- Interpreting the **show interface** command
- The **traceroute** command
- The **show controllers** command
- **debug** Commands
- Using time stamps

Viewing the Routing Table

Router#**show ip route**	Displays entire routing table
Router#**show ip route** *protocol*	Displays table about a specific *protocol* (for example, RIP or IGRP)
Router#**show ip route** *w.x.y.z*	Displays info about route *w.x.y.z*
Router#**show ip route connected**	Displays table of connected routes
Router#**show ip route static**	Displays table of static routes

Determining the Gateway of Last Resort

`Router(config)#ip default-network w.x.y.z`	Sets network *w.x.y.z* to be the default route. All routes not in the routing table will be sent to this network
`Router(config)#ip route 0.0.0.0 0.0.0.0` `172.16.20.1`	Specifies that all routes not in the routing table will be sent to 172.16.20.1

NOTE: You must use the **ip default-network** command with IGRP. Although you can use it with EIGRP or RIP, it is not recommended. Use the **ip route 0.0.0.0 0.0.0.0** command instead.

Routers that use the **ip default-network** command must have either a specific route to that network or a **0.0.0.0 /0** default route

Determining the Last Routing Update

`Router#show ip route`	Displays the entire routing table
`Router#show ip route w.x.y.z`	Displays info about route *w.x.y.z*
`Router#show ip protocols`	Displays IP routing protocol parameters and statistics
`Router#show ip rip database`	Displays the RIP database

OSI Layer 3 Testing

`Router#ping w.x.y.z`	Checks for Layer 3 connectivity with device at address *w.x.y.z*
`Router#ping`	Enters extended ping mode, which provides more options

TIP: See Part II, "CCNA 2," Chapter 4, "Learning About Other Devices," for output of an extended **ping** command.

OSI Layer 7 Testing

NOTE: See Part II, "CCNA 2," Chapter 4 for all applicable Telnet commands.

`Router#`**`debug telnet`**	Displays Telnet negotiation process
Interpreting the **show interface** command:	
`Router#`**`show interface serial 0/0`**	Displays status and stats of interface
`Serial 0/0 is` *up*`, line protocol is` *up*	First part refers to physical status. Second part refers to logical status
`...<output cut>...`	
Possible output results:	
`Serial 0/0 is up, line protocol is up`	Interface is up and working
`Serial 0/0 is up, line protocol is down`	Keepalive or connection problem (no clock rate, bad encapsulation)
`Serial 0/0 is down, line protocol is down`	Interface problem, or other end has not been configured
`Serial 0/0 is administratively down, line protocol is down`	Interface is disabled—shut down
`Router#`**`clear counters`**	Resets all interface counters to 0
`Router#`**`clear counters`** *`interface type/slot`*	Resets specific interface counters to 0

Using CDP to Troubleshoot

See Part II, "CCNA 2," Chapter 4, for all applicable CDP commands.

traceroute Command

Router#**trace** *w.x.y.z*	Displays all routes used to reach the destination of *w.x.y.z*

show controllers Command

Router#**show controllers serial 0/0**	Displays the type of cable plugged into the serial interface (DCE or DTE) and what the clock rate is, if it was set

debug Commands

Router#**debug all**	Turns on all possible debugging
Router#**u all** (short form of **undebug all**)	Turns off all possible debugging
Router#**show debug**	Lists what **debug** commands are on
Router#**terminal monitor**	Debug output will now be seen through a Telnet session (default is to only send output on console screen)
Router(config)#**service timestamps**	Adds a time stamp to all system logging messages
Router(config)#**service timestamps debug**	Adds a time stamp to all debugging messages
Router(config)#**service timestamps debug uptime**	Adds a time stamp along with total uptime of router to all debugging messages
Router(config)#**service timestamps debug datetime localtime**	Adds a time stamp displaying local time and date to all debugging messages
Router(config)#**no service timestamps**	Disables all time stamps

CAUTION: Turning all possible debugging on is extremely CPU intensive, and will probably cause your router to crash. Use *extreme caution* if you try this on a production device. Instead, be selective in which **debug** commands you turn on.

Do not leave debugging turned on. After you have gathered the necessary information from debugging, turn all debugging off.

TIP: Make sure you have the date and time set with the **clock** command at privileged mode so that the time stamps will mean more.

CHAPTER 10

Intermediate TCP/IP

This chapter provides information and commands concerning the following topics:

- Enabling the HTTP server
- Using the **netstat** command

ip http server Command

Router(config)#`ip http server`	Enables the HTTP server, including the Cisco web browser user interface
Router(config-if)#`no ip http server`	Disables the HTTP server

> **CAUTION:** The HTTP server was introduced in Cisco IOS Software Release 11.0 to extend router management to the web. You have limited management capabilities to your router through a web browser if the **ip http server** command is turned on.
>
> Do not turn on the **ip http server** command unless you plan on using the browser interface for the router. Having it on creates a potential security hole, because another port is open.

netstat Command

C\>`netstat`	Used in Windows and UNIX/Linux to display TCP/IP connection and protocol information. Used at the command prompt in Windows

CHAPTER 11

Access Control Lists (ACLs)

This chapter provides information and commands concerning the following topics:

- The numbers assigned to the different types of access control lists (ACLs)
- The use of wildcard masks in ACLs
- The **any** and **host** keywords used by ACLs
- How to create, apply, verify, and remove standard IP ACLs
- How to create, apply, verify, and remove extended IP ACLs
- How to create named ACLs
- How to restrict virtual terminal access

Access List Numbers

1–99 or 1300–1999	Standard IP
100–199 or 2000–2699	Extended IP
600–699	AppleTalk
800–899	IPX
900–999	Extended IPX
1000–1099	IPX Service Advertising Protocol

Wildcard Masks

When compared to an IP address, a wildcard mask will identify what addresses get filtered out in an access list:

- A 0 (zero) in a wildcard mask means to check the corresponding bit in the address for an exact match.
- A 1 (one) in a wildcard mask means to ignore the corresponding bit in the address—can be either 1 or 0.

Example 1: 172.16.0.0 0.0.255.255

172.16.0.0   =   10101100.00010000.00000000.00000000
0.0.255.255 =   00000000.00000000.11111111.11111111

Result   =   10101100.00010000.xxxxxxxx.xxxxxxxx
172.16.x.x (anything between 172.16.0.0 and 172.16.255.255)

TIP: An octet of all zeros means that the address has to match the address in the ACL exactly. An octet of all ones means that the address can be ignored.

Example 2: 172.16.8.0 0.0.7.255

172.168.8.0   =   10101100.00010000.00001000.00000000
0.0.0.7.255   =   00000000.00000000.00000111.11111111

Result   =   10101100.00010000.00001xxx.xxxxxxxx
00001*xxx*   =   00001*000* to 00001*111*   =   8–15
xxxxxxxx   =   00000000 to 11111111   =   0–255
Anything between 172.16.8.0 and 172.16.15.255

ACL Keywords

any	Used in place of 0.0.0.0 255.255.255.255, will match any address that it is compared against
host	Used in place of 0.0.0.0 in the wildcard mask; this will match only one specific address

Creating Standard ACLs

`Router(config)#access-list 10 permit` `172.16.0.0 0.0.255.255`	Read this line to say: All packets with a source IP address of 172.16.x.x will be permitted to continue through the internetwork
`access-list`	ACL command
`10`	Arbitrary number between 1 and 99, designating this as a standard IP ACL

`permit`	Packets that match this statement will be allowed to continue
`172.16.0.0`	Source IP address to be compared to
`0.0.255.255`	Wildcard mask
`Router(config)#access-list 10 deny host 172.17.0.1`	Read this line to say: All packets with a source IP address of 172.17.0.1 will be dropped and discarded
`access-list`	ACL command
`10`	Number between 1 and 99, designating this as a standard IP ACL
`deny`	Packets that match this statement will be dropped and discarded
`host`	Keyword
`172.17.0.1`	Specific host address
`Router(config)#access-list 10 permit any`	Read this line to say: All packets with any source IP address will be permitted to continue through the internetwork
`access-list`	ACL command
`10`	Number between 1 and 99, designating this as a standard IP ACL
`permit`	Packets that match this statement will be allowed to continue
`any`	Keyword to mean all IP addresses

TIP: There is an **implicit deny** statement that is hard coded into every ACL. You cannot see it, but it states "deny everything." This is always the last line of any ACL. If you want to defeat this implicit deny, put a **permit any** statement in your standard ACLs or **permit ip any any** in your extended ACLs as the last line.

Applying a Standard ACL to an Interface

`Router(config)#int fa0/0`	
`Router(config-if)#ip access-group 10 in`	Takes all access list lines that are defined as being part of group 10 and applies them in an inbound manner. Packets going into the router from FA0/0 will be checked

TIP: Access lists can be applied in either an inbound direction (keyword **in**) or in an outbound direction (keyword **out**).

Verifying ACLs

`Router#show ip interface`	Displays any ACLs applied to that interface
`Router#show access-lists`	Displays contents of all ACLs on the router
`Router#show access-list` *access-list-number*	Displays contents of ACL by the number specified
`Router#show access-list` *name*	Displays contents of ACL by the *name* specified
`Router#show run`	Displays all ACLs and interface assign-ments

Removing An ACL

`Router(config)#no access-list 10`	Removes **all** ACLs numbered 10

Creating Extended ACLs

`Router(config)#access-list 110 permit tcp 172.16.0.0 0.0.0.255 192.168.100.0 0.0.0.255 eq 80`	Read this line to say: HTTP packets with a source IP address of 172.16.0.x will be permitted to travel to destination address of 192.168.100.x
`access-list`	ACL command
`110`	Number is between 100 and 199, designat-ing this as an extended IP ACL
`permit`	Packets that match this statement will be allowed to continue
`tcp`	Protocol must be TCP
`172.16.0.0`	Source IP address to be compared to
`0.0.0.255`	Wildcard mask
`192.168.100.0`	Destination IP address to be compared to
`0.0.0.255`	Wildcard mask
`eq`	Operand, means "equal to"
`80`	Port 80, indicating HTTP traffic
`Router(config)#access-list 110 deny tcp any 192.168.100.7 0.0.0.0 eq 23`	Read this line to say: Telnet packets with any source IP address will be dropped if they are addressed to specific host 192.168.100.7
`access-list`	ACL command

`110`	Number is between 100 and 199, designat-ing this as an extended IP ACL
`deny`	Packets that match this statement will be dropped and discarded
`tcp`	Protocol must be TCP protocol
`any`	Any source IP address
`192.168.100.7`	Destination IP address to be compared to
`0.0.0.0`	Wildcard mask; address must match exactly
`eq`	Operand, means "equal to"
`23`	Port 23, indicating Telnet traffic

Applying an Extended ACL to an Interface

`Router(config)#int fa0/0` `Router(config-if)#ip access-group 110 out`	Takes all access list lines that are defined as being part of group 110 and applies them in an out-bound manner. Packets going out FA0/0 will be checked

TIP: Access lists can be applied in either an inbound direction (keyword **in**) or in an outbound direction (keyword **out**).

Creating Named ACLs

`Router(config)#ip access-list extended` `serveraccess`	Creates an extended named ACL called serveraccess

`Router(config-ext-nacl)#`**`permit tcp any host`** **`131.108.101.99 eq smtp`**	Permits mail packets from any source to reach host 131.108.101.99
`Router(config-ext-nacl)#`**`permit udp any host`** **`131.108.101.99 eq domain`**	Permits DNS packets from any source to reach host 131.108.101.99
`Router(config-ext-nacl)#`**`deny ip any any log`**	Denies all other packets from going any-where. If any packets do get denied, then log the results for me to look at later
`Router(config-ext-nacl)#`**`exit`**	
`Router(config)#`**`int fa 0/0`** `Router(config-if)#`**`ip access-group serveraccess`** **`out`**	Applies this ACL to the Fast Ethernet inter-face 0/0 in an outbound direction

Restricting Virtual Terminal Access

`Router(config)#`**`access-list 2 permit host`** **`172.16.10.2`**	Permits host 172.16.10.2 to Telnet into this router (see line 4 of this ACL)
`Router(config)#`**`access-list 2 permit 172.16.20.0`** **`0.0.0.255`**	Permits anyone from the 172.16.20.x address range to Telnet into this router (see line 4 of this ACL)
`Router(config)#`**`line vty 0 4`**	Denies all other Telnet requests (because of the implicit deny)
`Router(config-line)`**`access-class 2 in`**	Applies this ACL to all five vty virtual inter-faces

Configuration Example: Access Control Lists

Figure 11-1 shows the network topology for the configuration that follows, which shows five ACL examples using the commands covered in this chapter.

Figure 11-1   Network Topology for ACL Configuration

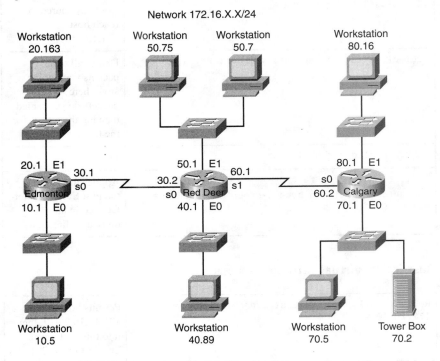

Example 1: Write an ACL that prevents the 10.0 network from accessing the 40.0 network, but everyone else can.

RedDeer(config)#`access-list 10 deny 172.16.10.0` `0.0.0.255`	Standard ACL denies complete network for complete TCP/IP suite of protocols
RedDeer(config)#`access-list 10 permit any`	Defeats the implicit deny
RedDeer(config)#`int e0`	
RedDeer(config)#`ip access-group 10 out`	Applies ACL in an outbound direction

Example 2: Write an ACL which states that 10.5 cannot access 50.7. Everyone else can.

Edmonton(config)#`access list 115 deny ip host` `172.16.10.5 host 172.16.50.7`	Extended ACL denies specific host for entire TCP/IP suite
Edmonton(config)#`access list 115 permit ip any` `any`	All others permitted through
Edmonton(config)#`int e0`	
Edmonton(config)#`ip access-group 115 in`	Applies ACL in an inbound direction

Example 3: Write an ACL which states that 10.5 can Telnet to the Red Deer router. No one else can.

RedDeer(config)#`access-list 20 permit host` `172.16.10.5`	
RedDeer(config)#`line vty 0 4`	Go to virtual terminal lines
RedDeer(config-line)#`access-class 20 in`	Use **access-class**, not **access-group**

Example 4: Write an ACL which states that 20.163 can Telnet to 70.2. No one else from 20.0 can Telnet to 70.2. Any other host from any other subnet can connect to 70.2 using anything that is available.

Calgary(config)#`access list 150 permit tcp host` `172.16.20.163 host 172.16.70.2 eq 23`	
Calgary(config)#`access list 150 deny tcp` `172.16.20.0 0.0.0.255 host 172.16.70.2 eq 23`	
Calgary(config)#`access list 150 permit ip any any`	Defeats the implicit deny
Calgary(config)#`int e0`	
Calgary(config)#`ip access-group 150 out`	

Example 5: Write an ACL which states that 50.1–50.63 are not allowed web access to 80.16. Hosts 50.64–50.254 are. Everyone can do everything else.

RedDeer(config)#`access-list 101 deny tcp` `172.16.50.0 0.0.0.63 host 172.16.80.16 eq 80`	
RedDeer(config)#`access-list 101 permit ip any any`	Allows device to do everything, including Telnet

`RedDeer(config)#int e1`	
`RedDeer(config)#ip access-group 101 in`	

Configuration Example: CCNA 2

Figure 11-2 shows the network topology for a three-router internetwork. The configurations of the three routers follow.

Figure 11-2   Three-Router Internetwork

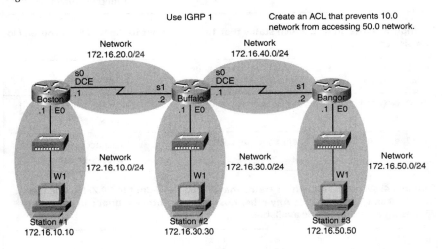

Boston Router

`Router>en`	Enters privileged mode
`Router#clock set 10:30:00 15 Nov 2004`	Sets local time on router
`Router#config t`	Enters global config mode
`Router(config)#hostname Boston`	Sets router name to **Boston**
`Boston(config)#no ip domain-lookup`	Turns off name resolution on unrecognized commands (spelling mistakes)

Boston(config)#**banner motd #** **This is the Boston Router.** **Authorized Access Only** **#**	Creates an MOTD banner
Boston(config)#**clock timezone EST -5**	Sets time zone to Eastern Standard Time (5 hours behind UTC)
Boston(config)#**enable secret cisco**	Enable secret password set to **cisco**
Boston(config)#**service password-encryption**	Passwords will be given weak encryption
Boston(config)#**line con 0**	Enters line console mode
Boston(config-line)#**logging sync**	Commands will be appended to a new line if interrupted by unsolicited messages
Boston(config-line)#**password class**	Sets password to **class**
Boston(config-line)#**login**	Enables password checking at login
Boston(config-line)#**exec-timeout 0 0**	Router will not log itself out
Boston(config-line)#**line vty 0 4**	Moves to virtual terminal lines 0 through 4
Boston(config-line)#**password class**	Sets password to **class**
Boston(config-line)#**login**	Enables password checking at login
Boston(config-line)#**line aux 0**	Moves to line auxiliary mode
Boston(config-line)#**password class**	Sets password to **class**
Boston(config-line)#**login**	Enables password checking at login

`Boston(config-line)#exit`	Moves back to global config mode
`Boston(config)#no service password-encryption`	Turns off password encryption
`Boston(config)#int E0`	Moves to Ethernet 0
`Boston(config-if)#desc Engineering LAN`	Sets locally significant description of the interface
`Boston(config-if)#ip address 172.16.10.1 255.255.255.0`	Assigns IP address and subnet mask to interface
`Boston(config-if)#no shut`	Turns on interface
`Boston(config-if)#int s0`	Moves directly to Serial 0 mode
`Boston(config-if)#desc Link to Buffalo Router`	Sets locally significant description of the interface
`Boston(config-if)#ip address 172.16.20.1 255.255.255.0`	Assigns IP address and subnet mask to interface
`Boston(config-if)#clock rate 56000`	Sets a clock rate for serial transmission (DCE cable must be plugged into this interface)
`Boston(config-if)#no shut`	Turns on interface
`Boston(config-if)#exit`	Moves back to global config mode
`Boston(config)#ip host buffalo 172.16.20.2`	Sets a local host name resolution to IP address 172.16.20.2
`Boston(config)#ip host bangor 172.16.40.2`	Sets a local host name resolution to IP address 172.16.40.2

`Boston(config)#`**`router igrp 1`**	Turns on IGRP routing process
`Boston(config-router)#`**`network 172.16.0.0`**	Tells router on which interfaces to run IGRP
`Boston(config-router)#`**`exit`**	Moves back to global config mode
`Boston(config)#`**`exit`**	Moves back to privileged mode
`Boston#`**`copy run start`**	Saves config to **NVRAM**

Buffalo Router

`Router>`**`en`**	Enters privileged mode
`Router#`**`clock set 10:45:00 15 Nov 2004`**	Sets local time on router
`Router#`**`config t`**	Enters global config mode
`Router(config)#`**`hostname Buffalo`**	Sets router name to **Buffalo**
`Buffalo(config)#`**`no ip domain-lookup`**	Turns off name resolution on unrecognized commands (spelling mistakes)
`Buffalo(config)#`**`banner motd #`** **`This is the Buffalo Router.`** **`Authorized Access Only`** **`#`**	Creates an MOTD banner
`Buffalo(config)#`**`clock timezone EST -5`**	Sets time zone to Eastern Standard Time (5 hours behind UTC)
`Buffalo(config)#`**`enable secret cisco`**	Enable secret password set to **cisco**
`Buffalo(config)#`**`service password-encryption`**	Passwords will be given weak encryption

`Buffalo(config)#`**`line con 0`**	Enters line console mode
`Buffalo(config-line)#`**`logging sync`**	Commands will be appended to a new line if interrupted by unsolicited messages
`Buffalo(config-line)#`**`password class`**	Sets password to **class**
`Buffalo(config-line)#`**`login`**	Enables password checking at login
`Buffalo(config-line)#`**`exec-timeout 0 0`**	Router will not log itself out
`Buffalo(config-line)#`**`line vty 0 4`**	Moves to virtual terminal lines 0 through 4
`Buffalo(config-line)#`**`password class`**	Sets password to **class**
`Buffalo(config-line)#`**`login`**	Enables password checking at login
`Buffalo(config-line)#`**`line aux 0`**	Moves to line auxiliary mode
`Buffalo(config-line)#`**`password class`**	Sets password to **class**
`Buffalo(config-line)#`**`login`**	Enables password checking at login
`Buffalo(config-line)#`**`exit`**	Moves back to global config mode
`Buffalo(config)#`**`no service password-encryption`**	Turns off password encryption
`Buffalo(config)#`**`int E0`**	Moves to Ethernet 0
`Buffalo(config-if)#`**`desc Sales LAN`**	Sets locally significant description of the interface
`Buffalo(config-if)#`**`ip address 172.16.30.1 255.255.255.0`**	Assigns IP address and subnet mask to interface

`Buffalo(config-if)#`**`no shut`**	Turns on interface
`Buffalo(config-if)#`**`int s0`**	Moves directly to Serial 0 mode
`Buffalo(config-if)#`**`desc Link to Bangor Router`**	Sets locally significant description of the interface
`Buffalo(config-if)#`**`ip address 172.16.40.1 255.255.255.0`**	Assigns IP address and subnet mask to interface
`Buffalo(config-if)#`**`clock rate 56000`**	Sets a clock rate for serial transmission (DCE cable must be plugged into this interface)
`Buffalo(config-if)#`**`no shut`**	Turns on interface
`Buffalo(config-if)#`**`int s1`**	Moves directly to Serial 1 mode
`Buffalo(config-if)#`**`desc Link to Boston Router`**	Sets locally significant description of the interface
`Buffalo(config-if)#`**`ip address 172.16.20.2 255.255.255.0`**	Assigns IP address and subnet mask to interface
`Buffalo(config-if)#`**`no shut`**	Turns on interface
`Buffalo(config-if)#`**`exit`**	Moves back to global config mode
`Buffalo(config)#`**`ip host boston 172.16.20.1`**	Sets a local host name resolution to IP address 172.16.20.1
`Buffalo(config)#`**`ip host bangor 172.16.40.2`**	Sets a local host name resolution to IP address 172.16.40.2
`Buffalo(config)#`**`router igrp 1`**	Turns on IGRP routing process

`Buffalo(config-router)#network 172.16.0.0`	Tells router on which interfaces to run IGRP
`Buffalo(config-router)#exit`	Moves back to global config mode
`Buffalo(config)#exit`	Moves back to privileged mode
`Buffalo#copy run start`	Saves config to NVRAM

Bangor Router

`Router>en`	Enters privileged mode
`Router#clock set 11:00:00 15 Nov 2004`	Sets local time on router
`Router#config t`	Enters global config mode
`Router(config)#hostname Bangor`	Sets router name to **Bangor**
`Bangor(config)#no ip domain-lookup`	Turns off name resolution on unrecognized commands (spelling mistakes)

`Bangor(config)#banner motd #`
`This is the Bangor Router.`
`Authorized Access Only`
`#`
	Creates an MOTD banner

`Bangor(config)#clock timezone EST -5`	Sets time zone to Eastern Standard Time (5 hours behind UTC)
`Bangor(config)#enable secret cisco`	Enable secret password set to **cisco**
`Bangor(config)#service password-encryption`	Passwords will be given weak encryption
`Bangor(config)#line con 0`	Enters line console mode

`Bangor(config-line)#`**`logging sync`**	Commands will be appended to a new line if interrupted by unsolicited messages
`Bangor(config-line)#`**`password class`**	Sets password to **class**
`Bangor(config-line)#`**`login`**	Enables password checking at login
`Bangor(config-line)#`**`exec-timeout 0 0`**	Router will not log itself out
`Bangor(config-line)#`**`line vty 0 4`**	Moves to virtual terminal lines 0 through 4
`Bangor(config-line)#`**`password class`**	Sets password to **class**
`Bangor(config-line)#`**`login`**	Enables password checking at login
`Bangor(config-line)#`**`line aux 0`**	Moves to line auxiliary mode
`Bangor(config-line)#`**`password class`**	Sets password to **class**
`Bangor(config-line)#`**`login`**	Enables password checking at login
`Bangor(config-line)#`**`exit`**	Moves back to global config mode
`Bangor(config)#`**`no service password-encryption`**	Turns off password encryption
`Bangor(config)#`**`int E0`**	Moves to Ethernet 0
`Bangor(config-if)#`**`desc Executive LAN`**	Sets locally significant description of the interface
`Bangor(config-if)#`**`ip address 172.16.50.1 255.255.255.0`**	Assigns IP address and subnet mask to interface
`Bangor(config-if)#`**`no shut`**	Turns on interface
`Bangor(config-if)#`**`int s1`**	Moves directly to Serial 1 mode

`Bangor(config-if)#desc Link to Buffalo Router`	Sets locally significant description of the interface
`Bangor(config-if)#ip address 172.16.40.2 255.255.255.0`	Assigns IP address and subnet mask to interface
`Bangor(config-if)#no shut`	Turns on interface
`Bangor(config-if)#exit`	Moves back to global config mode
`Bangor(config)#ip host buffalo 172.16.40.1`	Sets a local host name resolution to IP address 192.168.40.1
`Bangor(config)#ip host bangor 172.16.20.1`	Sets a local host name resolution to IP address 192.168.20.2
`Bangor(config)#router igrp 1`	Turns on IGRP routing process
`Bangor(config-router)#network 172.16.0.0`	Tells router on which interfaces to run IGRP
`Bangor(config-router)#exit`	Moves back to global config mode
`Bangor(config)#exit`	Moves back to privileged mode
`Bangor#copy run start`	Saves config to NVRAM

PART III

CCNA 3

PART III CCNA 3

CHAPTER 1

Introduction to Classless Routing

This chapter provides information and commands concerning the following topics:

- The **ip subnet-zero** command
- Mandatory and optional commands for configuring RIP Version 2 (RIP-2)

Variable-Length Subnet Masking (VLSM)

See Appendix B, "VLSM," for information on this topic.

Subnet Zero

`Router(config)#ip subnet-zero`	Allows the use of the all-0 subnets
`Router(config)#no ip subnet-zero`	Disables the use of the all-0 subnet

NOTE: With **ip subnet-zero** turned on, you now have the ability to use subnet-zero. Current common practice is to use the all-ones subnet when working with VLSM. Therefore, you no longer use the formula $2^N - 2$ for the number of valid subnets created, but rather use the formula 2^N, where N = number of bits borrowed.

The command **ip subnet-zero** is on by default in version Cisco IOS Software Release 12.0 and later.

RIP Version 2: Mandatory Commands

`Router(config)#router rip`	Turns on the RIP routing process; the same command as used for RIP Version 1 (RIP-1)
`Router(config-router)#version 2`	Turns on Version 2 of the routing process. Version 1 is default
`Router(config-router)#network w.x.y.z`	*w.x.y.z* is the network number of the *directly connected classful network* you want to advertise

RIP Version 2: Optional Commands

`Router(config-router)#no version 2`	Changes back to RIP-1
`Router(config-router)#version 1`	Changes RIP routing to RIP-1
`Router(config-router)#no auto-summary`	RIP-2 summarizes networks at the classful boundary. This command turns autosummarization off
`Router(config-router)#auto-summary`	Re-enables autosummarization at the classful boundary

NOTE: The optional commands covered in Part II, "CCNA 2," Chapter 7, "Distance Vector Routing Protocols," for RIP-1 also work on RIP-2.

NOTE: The verification commands covered in Part II, "CCNA 2," Chapter 7 for dynamic routing protocols also work on RIP-2.

NOTE: The troubleshooting commands covered in Part II, "CCNA 2," Chapter 7 for RIP-1 also work on RIP-2.

Configuration Example: RIP-2 Routing

Figure 1-1 shows the network topology for the configuration that follows, which shows how to configure RIP-2 using the commands covered in this chapter.

Figure 1-1   Network Topology for RIP-2 Routing Configuration

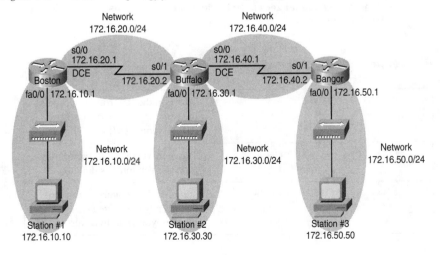

NOTE: The host name, password, and interfaces have all been configured as per the configuration example in Part II, "CCNA 2," Chapter 3, "Configuring a Router," of this book.

Boston Router

Boston>en	
Boston#config t	
Boston(config)#router rip	Enables RIP routing
Boston(config-router)#version 2	Enables RIP-2
Boston(config-router)#network 172.16.0.0	Advertises directly connected networks (classful address only)
Boston(config-router)#no auto-summary	Turns off autosummarization
Boston(config-router)#exit	
Boston(config)#exit	
Boston#copy run start	

Buffalo Router

Buffalo>en	
Buffalo#config t	
Buffalo(config)#router rip	Enables RIP routing
Buffalo(config-router)#version 2	Enables RIP-2
Buffalo(config-router)#network 172.16.0.0	Advertises directly connected networks (classful address only)
Buffalo(config-router)#no auto-summary	Turns off autosummarization
Buffalo(config-router)#Ctrl z	Exits back to privileged mode
Buffalo#copy run start	

Bangor Router

Bangor>en	

`Bangor#`**`config t`**	
`Bangor(config)#`**`router rip`**	Enables RIP routing
`Bangor(config-router)#`**`version 2`**	Enables RIP-2
`Bangor(config-router)#`**`network 172.16.0.0`**	Advertises directly connected networks (classful address only)
`Bangor(config-router)#`**`no auto-summary`**	Turns off autosummarization
`Bangor(config-router)#`[Ctrl][z]	Exits back to privileged mode
`Bangor#`**`copy run start`**	

CHAPTER 2

Single-Area OSPF

This chapter provides information and commands concerning the following Open Shortest Path First (OSPF) topics:

- Configuring single-area OSPF (mandatory commands)
- Using wildcard masks with OSPF areas
- Configuring single-area OSPF (optional commands), regarding
  — Loopback interfaces
  — DR/BDR election priority
  — Cost metrics
  — Authentication
  — Timers
  — Propagating a default route
- Verifying OSPF
- Troubleshooting OSPF

OSPF Routing: Mandatory Commands

Router(config)#**router ospf 123** Router(config-router)#	Turns on OSPF process number 123. The process ID is any value between 1–65535. The process ID *does not equal* the OSPF area
Router(config-router)#**network 172.16.10.0 0.0.0.255 area 0**	OSPF advertises interfaces, not networks. Uses the wildcard mask to determine which interfaces to advertise. Read this line to say: Any interface with an address of 172.16.10.x is to be put into Area 0

NOTE: The process ID number of one router does not have to match the process ID number of any other router. Unlike Interior Gateway Routing Protocol (IGRP) or Enhanced IGRP (EIGRP), matching this number across all routers does *not* ensure network adjacencies will form.

Using Wildcard Masks with OSPF Areas

`Router(config-router)#network 172.16.10.1 0.0.0.0 area 0`	Read this line to say: Any interface with an exact address of 172.16.10.1 is to be put into Area 0
`Router(config-router)#network 172.16.10.0 0.0.255.255 area 0`	Read this line to say: Any interface with an address of 172.16.x.x is to be put into Area 0
`Router(config-router)#network 0.0.0.0 255.255.255.255 area 0`	Read this line to say: Any interface with any address is to be put into Area 0

OSPF Routing: Optional Commands

Loopback Interfaces

`Router(config)#interface lo0`	Moves to virtual interface Loopback 0
`Router(config-if)#ip address 192.168.100.1 255.255.255.255`	Assigns IP address to interface

NOTE: Loopback interfaces are always "up and up" and do not go down. Great for using as an OSPF router ID.

OSPF DR/BDR Election

`Router(config)#int S0/0`	
`Router(config-if)#ip ospf priority 50`	Changes OSPF interface priority to 50

NOTE: The assigned priority can be between 0 and 255. A priority of 0 guarantees that the router never wins a designated router (DR) election, and 255 guarantees a tie in the election (tie broken by highest router ID). The default priority is 1.

Modifying OSPF Cost Metrics

`Router(config)#int s 0/0`	
`Router(config-if)#bandwidth 128`	By changing the bandwidth, OSPF will recalculate cost of link
or	
`Router(config-if)#ip ospf cost 1564`	Changes the cost to a value of 1564

NOTE: The cost of a link is determined by dividing the reference bandwidth by the interface bandwidth.

The reference bandwidth is 10^8.

Bandwidth is a number between 1–10000000 and is measured in kilobits.

Cost is a number between 1–65535. Cost has no unit of measurement—it is just a number.

OSPF Authentication: Simple

`Router(config)#router ospf 456`	
`Router(config-router)#area 0 authentication`	Turns on simple authentication— password sent in clear text
`Router(config-router)#exit`	
`Router(config)#int fa 0/0`	
`Router(config-if)#ip ospf authentication-key fred`	Sets key (password) to **fred**

OSPF Authentication Using MD5 Encryption

`Router(config)#router ospf 456`	
`Router(config-router)#area 0 authentication message-digest`	Enables authentication with MD5 password encryption
`Router(config-router)#exit`	
`Router(config)#int fa 0/0`	

`Router(config-if)#ip ospf message-digest-key 1` `md5 fred`	**1** is the *key-id.* This value must be the same as that of the neighboring router **md5** indicates that the MD5 hash algorithm will be used **fred** is the key (password) and must be the same as that of the neighboring router

OSPF Timers

`Router(config-if)#ip ospf hello-interval timer` `20`	Changes Hello timer to 20 seconds
`Router(config-if)#ip ospf dead-interval 80`	Changes Dead Interval timer to 80 seconds

NOTE: The Hello and Dead Interval timers must match for routers to become neighbors.

Propagating a Default Route

`Router(config)#ip route 0.0.0.0 0.0.0.0 s0/0`	Creates a default route
`Router(config)#router ospf 1`	
`Router(config-router)#default-information-` `originate`	Sets the default route to be propagated to all OSPF routers

Verifying OSPF Configuration

`Router#show ip protocol`	Displays parameters for all protocols running on router
`Router#show ip route`	Displays complete IP routing table
`Router#show ip ospf`	Displays basic information

Router#show ip ospf interface	Displays OSPF information as it relates to all interfaces
Router#show ip ospf int fa 0/0	Displays OSPF information for interface fa 0/0
Router#show ip ospf neighbor	Lists all OSPF neighbors and their states
Router#show ip ospf neighbor detail	Displays a detailed list of neighbors
Router#show ip ospf database	Displays contents of OSPF database

Troubleshooting OSPF

Router#clear ip route *	Clears entire routing table, forcing it to rebuild
Router#clear ip route a.b.c.d	Clears specific route to network a.b.c.d
Router#clear ip ospf counters	Resets OSPF counters
Router#clear ip ospf process	Resets entire OSPF process forcing OSPF to re-create neighbors, database, and routing table
Router#debug ip ospf events	Displays all OSPF events
Router#debug ip ospf adj	Displays various OSPF states and DR and BDR election between adjacent routers
Router#debug ip ospf packets	Displays OPSF packets

Configuration Example: Single-Area OSPF

Figure 2-1 shows the network topology for the configuration that follows, which shows a single-area OSPF network configuration using the commands covered in this chapter.

Figure 2-1   Network Topology for Single-Area OSPF Configuration

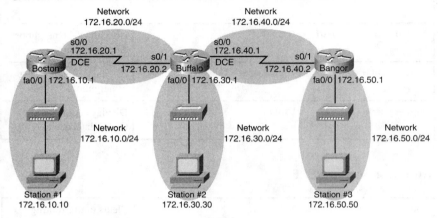

Boston Router

`Router>en`	
`Router#config t`	
`Router(config)#no ip domain-lookup`	Turns off DNS queries so that spelling mistakes will not slow you down
`Router(config)#hostname Boston`	Sets host name
`Boston(config)#line con 0`	
`Boston(config-line)#logging sync`	Commands interrupted by console messages will be appended to a new line
`Boston(config-line)#exit`	
`Boston(config)#int fa 0/0`	
`Boston(config-if)#ip add 172.16.10.1 255.255.255.0`	
`Boston(config-if)#no shut`	

Boston(config-if)#`int s0/0`	
Boston(config-if)#`ip add 172.16.20.1 255.255.255.0`	
Boston(config-if)#`clock rate 56000`	DCE cable connected to this interface
Boston(config-if)#`no shut`	
Boston(config-if)#`exit`	
Boston(config)#`router ospf 1`	Turns on OSPF process 1
Boston(config-router)#`net 172.16.10.0 0.0.0.255 area 0`	Any interface with address of 172.10.10.x will be part of Area 0
Boston(config-router)#`net 172.16.20.0 0.0.0.255 area 0`	Any interface with address of 172.16.20.x will be part of Area 0
Boston(config-router)#Ctrl z	
Boston#`copy run start`	

Buffalo Router

Router>`en`	
Router#`config t`	
Router(config)#`no ip domain-lookup`	Turns off DNS queries so that spelling mistakes will not slow you down
Router(config)#`hostname Buffalo`	Sets host name
Buffalo(config)#`line con 0`	
Buffalo(config-line)#`logging sync`	Commands interrupted by console mes-sages will be appended to a new line
Buffalo(config-line)#`exit`	
Buffalo(config)#`int fa 0/0`	

Buffalo(config-if)#**ip add 172.16.30.1 255.255.255.0**	
Buffalo(config-if)#**no shut**	
Buffalo(config-if)#**int s0/0**	
Buffalo(config-if)#**ip add 172.16.40.1 255.255.255.0**	
Buffalo(config-if)#**clock rate 56000**	DCE cable connected to this interface
Buffalo(config-if)#**no shut**	
Buffalo(config)#**int s 0/1**	
Buffalo(config-if)#**ip add 172.16.20.2 255.255.255.0**	
Buffalo(config-if)#**no shut**	
Buffalo(config-if)#**exit**	
Buffalo(config)#**router ospf 463**	Turns on OSPF process 463
Buffalo(config-router)#**net 172.16.0.0 0.0.255.255 area 0**	Any interface with address of 172.16.x.x will be part of Area 0
Buffalo(config-router)#Ctrl Z	
Buffalo#**copy run start**	

Bangor Router

Router>**en**	
Router#**config t**	
Router(config)#**no ip domain-lookup**	Turns off DNS queries so that spelling mistakes will not slow you down
Router(config)#**hostname Buffalo**	Sets host name
Bangor(config)#**line con 0**	

Bangor(config-line)#**logging sync**	Commands interrupted by console mes-sages will be appended to a new line
Bangor(config-line)#**exit**	
Bangor(config)#**int fa 0/0**	
Bangor(config-if)#**ip add 172.16.50.1 255.255.255.0**	
Bangor(config-if)#**no shut**	
Bangor(config)#**int s 0/1**	
Bangor(config-if)#**ip add 172.16.40.2 255.255.255.0**	
Bangor(config-if)#**no shut**	
Bangor(config-if)#**exit**	
Bangor(config)#**router ospf 100**	Turns on OSPF process 100
Bangor(config-router)#**net 172.16.40.2 0.0.0.0 area 0**	Interface with address of 172.16.40.2 will be part of Area 0
Bangor(config-router)#**net 172.16.50.1 0.0.0.0 area 0**	Interface with address of 172.16.50.1 will be part of Area 0
Bangor(config-router)#Ctrl z	
Bangor#**copy run start**	

CHAPTER 3

EIGRP

This chapter provides information and commands concerning the following topics:

- Configuring EIGRP
- EIGRP auto summarization
- Verifying EIGRP
- Troubleshooting EIGRP

Configuring EIGRP

`Router(config)#router eigrp 100`	Turns on the EIGRP process **100** is the autonomous system (AS) number, which can be a number between 1 and 65535 All routers in the same AS must use the same AS number
`Router(config-router)#network 10.0.0.0`	Specifies which network to advertise in EIGRP
`Router(config-router)#eigrp log-neighbor-changes`	Logs any changes to an EIGRP neighbor adjacency

TIP: The **eigrp log-neighbor-changes** command, although optional, is recommended to help with troubleshooting.

`Router(config-if)#bandwidth x`	Sets the bandwidth to match the interface's line speed
`Router(config-router)#no network 10.0.0.0`	Removes the network from the EIGRP process
`Router(config)#no eigrp 100`	Disables routing process 100

EIGRP Auto Summarization

`Router(config-router)#no auto-summary`	Turns off the auto-summarization feature. Networks are summarized at the classful boundary by default
`Router(config)#int fa 0/0`	
`Router(config-if)#ip summary-address eigrp 100 10.10.0.0 255.255.0.0`	Enables manual summarization on this specific interface for the given address and mask

> **CAUTION:** EIGRP automatically summarizes networks at the classful boundary. A poorly designed network with discontiguous subnets could have problems with connectivity if the summarization feature is left on. You could have two routers advertise the same network—172.16.0.0/16—when in fact the intention is for the routers to advertise two different networks—172.16.10.0/24 and 172.16.20.0/24.
>
> Recommended practice is that you turn off automatic summarization, use the **ip summary-address** command, and summarize manually what you need to.

Verifying EIGRP

`Router#show ip eigrp neighbors`	Displays a neighbor table
`Router#show ip eigrp neighbors detail`	Displays a detailed neighbor table
`Router#show ip eigrp interfaces`	Displays information for each interface
`Router#show ip eigrp int s 0/0`	Displays information for a specific interface
`Router#show ip eigrp int 100`	Displays information for interfaces running process 100
`Router#show ip eigrp topology`	Displays the topology table. This command will show you where your feasible successors are
`Router#show ip eigrp traffic`	Displays the number and type of packets sent and received

Troubleshooting EIGRP

Router#`debug eigrp fsm`	Displays events/actions related to the DUAL FSM
Router#`debug eigrp packet`	Displays events/actions related to EIGRP packets
Router#`debug eigrp neighbor`	Displays events/actions related to EIGRP neighbors

Configuration Example: EIGRP

Figure 3-1 shows the network topology for the configuration that follows, which shows how to configure EIGRP using the commands covered in this chapter.

Figure 3-1   Network Topology for EIGRP Configuration

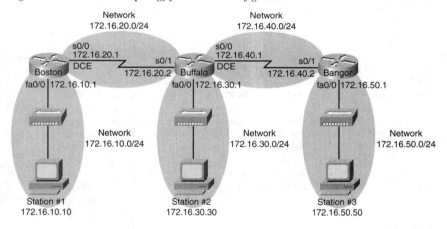

NOTE: The host name, password, and interfaces have all been configured as per the configuration example in the Part II, "CCNA 2," Chapter 3, "Configuring a Router."

Boston Router

Boston>`en`	
Boston#`config t`	
Boston(config)#`router eigrp 100`	Enables EIGRP routing

`Boston(config-router)#no auto-summary`	Disables auto summarization
`Boston(config-router)#eigrp log-neighbor-changes`	Changes with neighbors will be displayed
`Boston(config-router)#network 172.16.0.0`	Advertises directly connected networks (classful address only)
`Boston(config-router)#exit`	
`Boston(config)#exit`	
`Boston#copy run start`	

Buffalo Router

`Buffalo>en`	
`Buffalo#config t`	
`Buffalo(config)#router eigrp 100`	Enables EIGRP routing
`Buffalo(config-router)#no auto-summary`	Disables auto summarization
`Buffalo(config-router)#eigrp log-neighbor-changes`	Changes with neighbors will be displayed
`Buffalo(config-router)#network 172.16.0.0`	Advertises directly connected networks (classful address only)
`Buffalo(config-router)#`Ctrl Z	Exits back to privileged mode
`Buffalo#copy run start`	

Bangor Router

`Bangor>en`	
`Bangor#config t`	

Bangor(config)#**router eigrp 100**	Enables EIGRP routing
Bangor(config-router)#**no auto-summary**	Disables auto summarization
Bangor(config-router)#**eigrp log-neighbor-changes**	Changes with neighbors will be displayed
Bangor(config-router)#**network 172.16.0.0**	Advertises directly connected networks (classful address only)
Bangor(config-router)#⟦Ctrl⟧⟦z⟧	Exits back to privileged mode
Bangor#**copy run start**	

Switching Concepts

There are no commands affiliated with this module of CCNA 3 as covered in the Cisco Networking Academy Program curriculum.

There are no commands affiliated with this module of CCNA 3 as covered in the Cisco Networking Academy Program curriculum.

Switch Configuration

This chapter provides information and commands concerning the following topics:

- Configuring a switch (1900/2900/2950 Series), including
  - Host names
  - Passwords
  - IP addresses and default gateways
  - Interface descriptions
  - Duplex and speed settings
  - Working with the MAC address table
  - Port security
- Resetting switch configurations (1900/2900/2950 series)
- Upgrading firmware
- Backing up/restoring/upgrading IOS using a TFTP server
- Password recovery procedures

> **TIP:** The 1900 series switch uses an interactive menu system. Selecting different letters from the menu will take you to different places in the operating system. For this book, and for a better control of the 1900 series switch, select the command-line option by pressing the letter Ⓚ to get to the user mode prompt >.

Help Commands

`switch>?`	The ? works here the same as in a router

Command Modes

`switch>enable`	User mode, same as a router
`switch#`	Privileged mode
`switch#disable`	Leaves privileged mode
`switch>exit`	Leaves user mode

Verifying Commands

switch#`show version`	Displays information on software and hardware
switch#`show flash:`	Displays information on Flash memory (for the 2900/2950 series only)
switch#`show mac-address-table`	Displays current MAC address forwarding table
switch#`show controllers ethernet-controller`	Displays information about Ethernet controller
switch#`show running-config`	Displays current configuration in DRAM
switch#`show start`	Displays current configuration in NVRAM
switch#`show post`	Displays whether the switch passed POST
switch#`show vlan`	Displays the current VLAN config-uration
switch#`show interfaces`	Displays interface config-uration and status of line: up/up, up/down, admin down
switch#`show interface vlan1`	Displays setting of virtual interface VLAN 1, the default VLAN on the switch

Resetting Switch Configuration

1900 Series Switch

1900switch#`delete vtp`	Removes VLAN Trunking Protocol (VTP) information
1900switch#`delete nvram`	Resets switch back to factory defaults
1900switch>`en`	
1900switch#`reload`	Restarts the switch

2900/2950 Series Switch

switch#**delete flash:vlan.dat**	Removes VLAN database from Flash memory
Delete filename [vlan.dat]?	Press ⏎Enter
Delete flash:vlan.dat? [confirm]	Reconfirm by pressing ⏎Enter
Switch#**erase startup-config**	Erases file from NVRAM
<output omitted>	
Switch#**reload**	Restarts the switch

Setting Host Names

1900 Series Switch

#**config t**	
(config)#**hostname 1900Switch**	Same method as the router
1900Switch(config)#	

2900/2950 Series Switch

Switch#**config t**	
Switch(config)#**hostname 2900Switch**	Same method as the router
2900Switch(config)#	

Setting Passwords: 1900 Series Switches

1900Switch(config)#**enable password level 1 cisco**	Sets the user mode password to **cisco**
1900Switch(config)#**enable password level 15 class**	Sets the enable mode password to **class**
1900Switch(config)#**enable secret scott**	Sets the enable secret password to **scott**

TIP: The user mode password is what you need to enter to move from the menu system to the CLI. The enable mode password is what you use to move from user mode to privileged mode.

Setting Passwords: 2900/2950 Series Switches

Setting passwords for the 2900/2950 series switches is the same method as used for a router.

`2900Switch(config)#enable password cisco`	Sets enable password to **cisco**
`2900Switch(config)#enable secret class`	Sets encrypted secret password to class
`2900Switch(config)#line con 0`	Enters line console mode
`2900Switch(config-line)#login`	Enables password checking
`2900Switch(config-line)#password cisco`	Sets password to **cisco**
`2900Switch(config-line)#exit`	Exits line console mode
`2900Switch(config-line)#line aux 0`	Enters line auxiliary mode
`2900Switch(config-line)#login`	Enables password checking
`2900Switch(config-line)#password cisco`	Sets password to **cisco**
`2900Switch(config-line)#exit`	Exits line auxiliary mode
`2900Switch(config-line)#line vty 0 4`	Enters line vty mode for all five virtual ports
`2900Switch(config-line)#login`	Enables password checking
`2900Switch(config-line)#password cisco`	Sets password to **cisco**
`2900Switch(config-line)#exit`	Exits line vty mode
`2900Switch(config)#`	

Setting IP Address and Default Gateway

1900 Series Switch

`1900Switch(config)#ip address 172.16.10.2 255.255.255.0`	Sets the IP address and mask to allow for remote access to the switch

`1900Switch(config)#`**`ip default-gateway`** **`172.16.10.1`**	Sets the default gateway address to allow IP information an exit to the local network
`1900Switch(config)#`	

2900/2950 Series Switch

`2900Switch(config)#`**`int vlan1`**	Enters virtual interface for VLAN 1, the default VLAN on the switch
`2900Switch(config-if)#`**`ip address 172.16.10.2`** **`255.255.255.0`**	Sets the IP address and mask to allow for remote access to the switch
`2900Switch(config-if)#`**`exit`**	
`2900Switch(config)#`**`ip default-gateway`** **`172.16.10.1`**	To allow IP information an exit to the local network

TIP: For the 2900/2950 series switches, the IP address of the switch is just that—the IP address for the *entire* switch. That is why you set the address in VLAN 1—the default VLAN of the switch—and not in a specific Ethernet interface

Setting Interface Descriptions

1900 Series Switch

`1900Switch(config-if)#`**`description Finance VLAN`**	Adds description of interface

2900/2950 Series Switch

`2900Switch(config)#`**`int fa0/1`**	Enters interface mode
`2900Switch(config-if)#`**`description Finance VLAN`**	Adds description of interface

TIP: The 1900 series switch has either 12 or 24 Ethernet ports named e0/1, e0/2, …e0/24. There is also an Ethernet port named e0/25 that is in the back of the switch using an AUI interface. Ports A and B on the front of the switch are named fa0/26 and fa0/27, respectively. Ports A and B are Fast Ethernet.

TIP: The 2900 and 2950 series switches have either 12 or 24 Fast Ethernet ports named fa0/1, fa0/2, ...fa0/24.

Setting Duplex Settings: 1900 or 2900/2950 Series Switches

1900Switch(config)#int e0/1	Use e0/1 on 2900/2950
1900Switch(config-if)#duplex full	Forces full-duplex operation
1900Switch(config-if)#duplex auto	Enables auto-duplex config
1900Switch(config-if)#duplex half	Forces half-duplex operation

Setting Speed Settings: 2900/2950 Series Switches

2900Switch(config)#int fa0/1	
2900Switch(config-if)#speed 10	Forces 10-Mbps operation
2900Switch(config-if)#speed 100	Forces 100-Mbps operation
2900Switch(config-if)#speed auto	Enables autospeed configuration

Setting Web-Based Interface for Configuration: 1900 and 2900/2950 Series Switches

X900Switch(config)#ip http server	Turns on HTTP service
X900Switch(config)#ip http port 80	Sets port number for HTTP. This port should be turned off for security reasons unless it is being used

Managing the MAC Address Table: 1900 and 2900/2950 Series Switches

switch#`show mac-address-table`	Displays current MAC address forwarding table
switch#`clear mac-address-table`	Deletes all entries from current MAC address forwarding table
switch#`clear mac-address-table dynamic`	Deletes only dynamic entries from table

Configuring Static MAC Addresses

1900 Series Switch

1900Switch(config)#`mac-address-table permanent` *aaaa.aaaa.aaaa* `e0/1`	Sets a permanent address of *aaaa.aaaa.aaaa* in the MAC address table for interface e0/1
1900switch#`clear mac-address-table perm`	Deletes all permanent entries

2900/2950 Series Switch

2900Switch(config)#`mac-address-table static` *aaaa.aaaa.aaaa* `fa0/1 vlan 1`	Sets a permanent address to fa0/1 in VLAN 1
2900Switch(config)#`no mac-address-table static` *aaaa.aaaa.aaaa* `fa0/1 vlan 1`	Removes permanent address to fa0/1 in VLAN 1

Port Security: 1900 Series Switches

1900 Series Switch

1900Switch(config-if)#`port secure`	Interface will become secure
1900Switch(config-if)#`port secure max-mac-count 1`	Only one MAC address will be allowed in the MAC table for this interface

2900 Series Switch

`2900Switch(config)#int fa0/1`	
`2900Switch(config-if)#port security`	
`2900Switch(config-if)#port security max-mac-count 1`	Only one MAC address will be allowed for this interface
`2900Switch(config-if)#port security action shutdown`	Port will shut down if violation occurs

2950 Series Switch

`2950Switch(config)#int fa 0/1`	
`2950Switch(config-if)#switchport port-security`	
`2950Switch(config-if)#switchport port-security mac-address sticky`	Interface converts all MAC addresses to sticky secure addresses—only the MAC address learned first will now be accepted on this port
`2950Switch(config-if)#switchport port-security maximum 1`	Only one MAC address will be allowed for this interface
`2950Switch(config-if)#switchport port-security violation shutdown`	Port will shut down if violation occurs

Verifying Port Security

1900 Series Switch

`1900Switch#show mac-address-table security`	Displays the MAC address table with security information

2900/2950 Series Switch

`2900Switch#show port security`	Displays the MAC address table with security information

Upgrading Catalyst 1900 Firmware with a TFTP Server

To upgrade the Catalyst 1900 series switch firmware with a TFTP server, you must use the interactive menu.

Select option **F** from main menu	F for firmware
Select option **S** from Firmware menu	S for TFTP server
Enter in address for TFTP server	
Select option **F** from Firmware menu	F for firmware upgrade filename
Enter name of firmware upgrade file	
Select option **T** from Firmware menu	Initiates TFTP upgrade
Switch will reset itself automatically and load new firmware	

Copying IOS to TFTP Server

2900 Series Switch

`2900Switch#`**`copy flash:c2900XL-hs-mz-`** **`112.8.10-SA6.bin tftp`**	Same procedure as with router
`Source filename [c2900XL-hs-mz-112.8.10-` `SA6.bin]?`	Just press ↵Enter
`Destination IP address or hostname [ ]` **`192.168.1.3`**	Address of TFTP server
`Destination filename [c2900XL-hs-mz-` `112.8.10-SA6.bin]?`	Just press ↵Enter
`!!!!!!!!!!!!!!!!!!!!!!!!!!!!!!!!!!!!!!!!!!!!!!!!!!!!` `!!!!!!!!!!!!!!!!!!!!!!!!!!!!!!!!!!!!!!!!!!!!!!!!!!!!` `!!!!!!!!!!!!!!!!!!!!!!!!!!!!!!!!!!!!!!!!!!!!!!!!!!!!` `!!!!!!!!!!!!!!!!!!!!!`	Each bang symbol = 1 datagram sent
`<output cut>`	
`1119104 bytes copied in 21.43 secs`	
`2900Switch#`	

2950 Series Switch

`2950Switch#`**`copy flash tftp`**	Same procedure as with router
`Source filename [ ]?` **`c2950-c3h2s-mz.120-`** **`5.3.WC.1.bin`**	
`Destination IP address or hostname [ ]` **`192.168.1.3`**	Address of TFTP server
`Destination filename [c2950-c3h2s-mz.120-` `5.3.WC.1.bin]?`	Just press ⏎Enter
`!!!!!!!!!!!!!!!!!!!!!!!!!!!!!!!!!!!!!!!!!!!!!!!` `!!!!!!!!!!!!!!!!!!!!!!!!!!!!!!!!!!!!!!!!!!!!!!!` `!!!!!!!!!!!!!!!!!!!!!!!!!!!!!!!!!!!!!!!!!!!!!!!` `!!!!!!!!!!!!!!!!!!!!!`	Each bang symbol = 1 datagram sent
`<output cut>`	
`1674921 bytes copied in 31.542 secs`	
`2950Switch#`	

Restoring/Upgrading IOS/Startup-Config from TFTP Server

The procedure is the same for a switch as it is for a router. See Part II, "CCNA 2," Chapter 5, "Managing Cisco IOS Software."

Password Recovery for 1900 Series Switches

Unplug the power supply from the back of the switch	
Press and hold the Mode button on the front of the switch	
Plug the switch back in	
Wait until the LED above port 1X goes out, and then release the Mode button	This allows you to access the Systems-Engineering menu, which is a diagnostic menu for troubleshooting issues
Press ⏎Enter to continue	

Press ⏎Enter to display the Systems-Engineering menu	Note which firmware version is on the switch

Password Recovery for
Firmware 1.10 or Later

Power-cycle the switch	Unplug, then plug the switch back in
After POST complete, you see the following:	
Do you wish to clear the passwords? [Y]es or [N]o	You have 10 seconds to respond
Enter **Y** to delete the password	
Assign a new password from either the menu console or the CLI	As per the section on assigning passwords in this chapter

To View the Password You Are Trying to Recover	**Valid on Firmware Between 1.10 and 3.02**
Unplug the power supply from the back of the switch	
Press and hold the Mode button on the front of the switch	
Plug the switch back in	
Wait until the LED above port 1X goes out, then release the Mode button	This allows you to access the Systems-Engineering menu, which is a diagnostic menu for troubleshooting issues
Press ⏎Enter to continue	
Press ⏎Enter	
Select **S** on the Diagnostic-Console Systems Engineering menu	
Select **V** on the System-Debug interface	Displays the management console password
Select **M** option on the Console Settings menu	

Password Recovery for Firmware 1.09 and Earlier

You must contact Cisco Technical Assistance Center (TAC)	
Make sure you have the switch serial number or MAC address of the switch	

Password Recovery for 2900/2950 Series Switches

Unplug the power supply from the back of the switch	
Press and hold the Mode button on the front of the switch	
Plug the switch back in	
Wait until the LED above port 1X goes out, then release the Mode button	For the 2900 series switch
or	
Wait until the STAT LED goes out, then release the Mode button	For the 2950 series switch
Issue the following commands:	
switch: **flash_init**	Initializes the Flash memory
switch: **load_helper**	
switch: **flash:**	Do not forget the colon. This displays what files are in Flash memory
switch: **rename flash:config.text flash:config.old**	The config.text file contains the password
switch: **boot**	Boots the switch
Type **n** to exit the initial configuration dialog	Takes you to user mode

switch>en	Enters privileged mode
switch#rename flash:config.old flash:config.text	Renames the file back to the original name
Destination filename [config.text]	Press ⏎Enter
switch#copy flash:config.text system:running-config	Copies config file into memory
768 bytes copied in 0.624 seconds	
2900Switch#	Config file is now reloaded
2900Switch#config t	Enters global configuration mode
2900Switch(config)#	
Proceed to change the passwords as needed	
2900Switch(config)#exit	
2900Switch#copy run start	Saves config with new passwords

Firmware Upgrade of Catalyst 2950 Series Switches

2950Switch#archive tar /x tftp:// 192.168.1.3/c2950-c3h2s-mz.120-5.3.WC.1.tar flash:	Extracts a new IOS image into Flash memory. The image c2950-c3h2s-mz.120-5.3.WC.1.tar must be on the TFTP server located at 192.168.1.3
2950Switch(config)#boot system flash c2950-c3h2s-mz.120-5.3.WC.1.bin	Switch will now boot to this IOS
2950Switch(config)#exit	
2950Switch#reload	Restarts the switch

> **NOTE:** Tape Archive (TAR) is a compression format used in the transfer of files. TAR is a UNIX utility.
>
> BIN is an abbreviation for the word *binary*. A binary (.bin) file is a file containing information in binary form.
>
> Because Cisco IOS Software was based originally on a UNIX platform, IOS images are *.bin* or *.tar* files

Configuration Example: 2900 Series Switch

Figure 6-1 shows the network topology for the basic configuration of a 2900 series switch using the commands covered in this chapter.

Figure 6-1   Network Topology for 2900 Series Switch Configuration

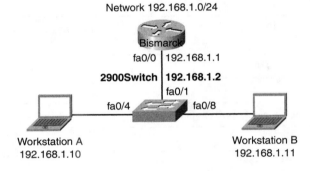

switch>en	Enters privileged mode
switch#config t	Enters global config mode
switch(config)#no ip domain-lookup	Turns off DNS queries so that spelling mistakes will not slow you down
switch(config)#hostname 2900	Sets host name
2900(config)#enable secret cisco	Sets encrypted secret password to **cisco**
2900(config)#line con 0	Enters line console mode
2900(config-line)#logging synchronous	Appends commands to new line; router information will not interrupt

`2900(config-line)#login`	User must log in to console before use
`2900(config-line)#password switch`	Sets password to **switch**
`2900(config-line)#exec-timeout 0 0`	Console will never log out
`2900(config-line)#exit`	Moves back to global config mode
`2900(config)#line aux 0`	Moves to line auxiliary mode
`2900(config-line)#login`	User must log in to auxiliary port before use
`2900(config-line)#password class`	Sets password to **class**
`2900(config-line)#exit`	Back to global config mode
`2900(config)#line vty 0 15`	Moves to configure all 16 vty ports at same time
`2900(config-line)#login`	User must log in to vty port before use
`2900(config-line)#password class`	Sets password to **class**
`2900(config-line)#exit`	Back to global config mode
`2900(config)#ip default-gateway 192.168.1.1`	Sets default gateway
`2900(config)#int vlan 1`	Moves to virtual interface VLAN 1
`2900(config-if)#ip add 192.168.1.2 255.255.255.0`	Sets IP address for switch
`2900(config-if)#no shut`	Turns virtual interface on
`2900(config-if)#int fa 0/1`	Moves to interface fa 0/1
`2900(config-if)#desc Link to Router`	Sets local description
`2900(config-if)#int fa 0/4`	Moves to interface fa 0/4
`2900(config-if)#desc Link to Workstation A`	Sets local description
`2900(config-if)#port security`	Activates port security

2900(config-if)#**port security max-mac-count 1**	Only one MAC address will be allowed in the MAC table
2900(config-if)#**port security action shutdown**	Port will be turned off if more than one MAC address is reported
2900(config-if)#**int fa 0/8**	Moves to interface fa 0/8
2900(config-if)#**desc Link to Workstation B**	Sets local description
2900(config-if)#**port security**	Activates port security
2900(config-if)#**port security max-mac-count 1**	Only one MAC address will be allowed in the MAC table
2900(config-if)#**port security action shutdown**	Port will be turned off if more than one MAC address is reported
2900(config-if)#**exit**	Returns to global config mode
2900(config)#**exit**	Returns to privileged mode
2900#**copy run start**	Saved configuration to NVRAM
2900#	

CHAPTER 7

Spanning Tree Protocol

This chapter provides information and commands concerning the following topics:

- Verifying the spanning-tree table of a switch
- Changing the spanning-tree priority of a switch
- Changing the Spanning Tree Protocol stage of a switch

Spanning-Tree Verification

Cisco IOS Software Release 12.0	Switch#**show spanning-tree brief**	Displays the spanning-tree table of the switch
Cisco IOS Software Release 12.1	Switch#**show spanning-tree**	Displays the spanning-tree table of the switch

Change Spanning-Tree Priority of a Switch

Cisco IOS Software Release 12.0	Switch(config)#**spanning-tree priority 1**	Number can be from 1–65535. Lower number means better chance of being elected the Root Bridge The default is 32768
Cisco IOS Software Release 12.1	Switch(config)#**spanning-tree vlan 1 priority 1**	Number can be from 1–65535. Lower number means better chance of being elected the Root Bridge The default is 32768

NOTE: In Cisco IOS Software Release 12.1, the priority is changed on a specific VLAN rather than on the switch itself.

Changing the Stage of Spanning Tree on an Interface

Switch(config)#int fa 0/1	
Switch(config-if)#spanning-tree portfast	See the Caution that follows

CAUTION: The command **spanning-tree portfast** forces a port to move directly to the Forwarding state, without having to transition from Blocking state to Listening, then Learning, and then finally Forwarding state. This can save up to 50 seconds of wait time. This is an excellent command on access ports that will never be hooked up to another switch (that is, ports connected to computers or other end devices, such as printers, servers, and so on). You must exercise caution with this command, however, because if a switch port is plugged into another switch and the **portfast** command is enabled, spanning tree will be defeated and a switching loop might be created.

CHAPTER 8

Virtual LANs

This chapter provides information and commands concerning the following topics for 1900, 2900, and 2950 series switches:

- Displaying VLAN information
- Creating static VLANs
- Assigning ports to VLANs
- Assigning ports using the **range** command (2950 series switch only)
- Saving VLAN configurations
- Erasing VLAN configurations
- Troubleshooting VLANs

Displaying VLAN Information

1900 Series Switch

1900Switch#**show vlan**	Shows VLAN information
1900Switch#**show vlan-membership**	Shows which ports belong to which VLAN
1900Switch#**show vlan 2**	Displays information about VLAN 2 only

2900/2950 Series Switch

2900Switch#**show vlan**	Shows all VLAN status
2900Switch#**show vlan brief**	Shows all VLAN status in brief
2900Switch#**show vlan id 2**	Displays information of VLAN 2 only
2900Switch#**show vlan name Marketing**	Displays information of VLAN named Marketing only

Creating Static VLANs

1900 Series Switch

1900Switch#**config t**	
1900Switch(config)#**vlan 2 name Engineering**	Creates VLAN 2 and names it Engineering
1900Switch(config)#**vlan 3 name Marketing**	Creates VLAN 3 and names it Marketing

2900 Series Switch

2900Switch#**vlan database**	Enters VLAN database mode
2900(vlan)#**vlan 2 name Engineering**	Creates VLAN 2 and names it Engineering
2900(vlan)#**vlan 3 name Marketing**	Creates VLAN 3 and names it Marketing
2900(vlan)#**exit**	Applies changes and exits VLAN database mode
2900#	

2950 Series Switch

2950Switch#**config t**	Enters global config mode
2950Switch(config)#**vlan 10**	Creates VLAN 10 and enters VLAN config mode for further definitions
2950Switch(config-vlan)#**name Accounting**	Assigns a name to a VLAN
2950Switch(config-vlan)#**exit**	Moves back to global config mode
2950Switch(config)#**vlan 20**	Creates VLAN 20 and enters VLAN config mode for further definitions
2950Switch(config-vlan)#**name Sales**	Assigns a name to a VLAN
2950Switch(config-vlan)#**exit**	Moves back to global config mode

TIP: For the 2900 series switch, you must apply the changes to the VLAN database for the changes to take effect. You can also use the command **apply** in the VLAN database, which will apply the changes, but not exit the mode. Using the ⒸⓉⓇⓁ Ⓩ command to exit out of the VLAN database will not apply the changes to the VLAN database.

TIP: For the 2950 series switch, the use of the VLAN database is being phased out, in favor of creating VLANs in the manner demonstrated in the preceding command syntax. If you use the **vlan database** command at the 2950Switch# prompt, the 2950 IOS will tell you this but will still allow you to use commands the same as the 2900 series switch. Get used to this style; it is the method to be used on all future releases of switches.

Assigning Ports to VLANs

1900 Series Switch

1900Switch#**config t**	
1900Switch(config)#**int e0/2**	Moves to interface mode
1900Switch(config-if)#**vlan static 2**	Assigns this port to VLAN 2
1900Switch(config-if)#**int e0/3**	Moves to interface mode
1900Switch(config-if)#**vlan static 3**	Assigns this port to VLAN 3
1900Switch(config-if)#**exit**	Exits interface mode
1900Switch(config)#	

2900/2950 Series Switch

2900Switch#**config t**	
2900Switch(config)#**int fa0/2**	Moves to interface mode
2900Switch(config-if)#**switchport mode access**	Sets switchport mode to access
2900Switch(config-if)#**switchport access vlan 2**	Assigns this port to VLAN 2
2900Switch(config-if)#**int fa0/3**	Moves to interface mode
2900Switch(config-if)#**switchport mode access**	Sets switchport mode to access

2900Switch(config-if)#**switchport access vlan 3**	Assigns this port to VLAN 3
2900Switch(config-if)#**exit**	Exits interface mode
2900Switch(config)#	

Assigning Ports Using the range Command (2950 Switch Only)

2950Switch(config)#**int range fa 0/1 - 4**	Enables you to set the same configuration parameters on multiple ports at the same time. Note that there is a space before and after the hyphen
2950Switch(config-if-range)#**switchport mode access**	Sets all ports to access mode
2950Switch(config-if-range)#**switchport access vlan 10**	Assigns all ports to VLAN 10

Saving VLAN Configurations

1900 Series Switch

Any command made to a 1900 series switch is automatically saved to NVRAM. There is no **copy run start** command on a 1900 series switch

2900/2950 Series Switch

Any command entered in the VLAN database is automatically saved as long as you leave the VLAN database properly with the **exit** command, and not (Ctrl)(z)

Router#**copy run start**	Saves the running-config to NVRAM

Erasing VLAN Configurations

1900 Series Switch

`1900Switch#`**`delete vtp`**	Deletes all VLAN information from the switch and resets VTP parameters to the factory defaults
Or:	
`1900Switch(config)#`**`int fa 0/2`**	
`1900Switch(config-if)#`**`no vlan static 2`**	Removes interface from VLAN 2 and puts it back into default VLAN 1
`1900Switch(config-if)#`**`exit`**	
`1900Switch(config)#`**`no vlan 2 name Engineering`**	Removes only VLAN 2 from database
`1900Switch(config)#`	

2900/2950 Series Switch

`2900Switch#`**`delete flash:vlan.dat`**	Removes entire VLAN database from Flash memory Make sure there is *no* space between the colon (:) and the characters **vlan.dat**. You can potentially erase the entire contents of Flash memory with this command if the syntax is not correct
`2900Switch#`**`delete flash:`**	
`Delete filename [ ]?` **`vlan.dat`**	Removes entire VLAN database from Flash memory
`Delete flash:vlan.dat? [confirm]`	Press the ⏎Enter key
`2900Switch#`	

Or:	
`2900Switch#`**`config t`**	
`2900Switch(config)#`**`int fa 0/3`**	
`2900Switch(config-if)#`**`no switchport access vlan 3`**	Removes port from VLAN 3 and reassigns it to default VLAN 1
`2900Switch(config-if)#`**`exit`**	
`2900Switch(config)#`**`exit`**	
`2900Switch#`**`vlan database`**	Enters VLAN database mode
`2900(vlan)#`**`no vlan 3`**	Removes only VLAN 2 from database
`2900(vlan)#`**`exit`**	Applies changes and exits VLAN database mode

NOTE: For the 1900 series switch, removing a VLAN from the database *does not* reassign ports in that VLAN back to the default Management VLAN. You must also go into the specific interface and reassign the ports as well.

NOTE: For any series switch, you cannot remove VLAN 1.

Troubleshooting VLANs

`2900Switch#`**`show vlan`**	Displays the complete VLAN database
`2900Switch#`**`show vlan brief`**	Displays a summary of the VLAN database
`2900Switch#`**`show interfaces`**	Displays a summary of each interface, including speed and duplex settings
`2900Switch#`**`debug sw-vlan packets`**	Displays information about VLAN packets a router has received but not capable of supporting

Configuration Example: 2900 Switch Configuration

Figure 8-1 shows the network topology for the configuration of VLANs on a 2900 series switch using the commands covered in this chapter.

Figure 8-1   Network Topology for VLAN Configuration on a 2900 Series Switch

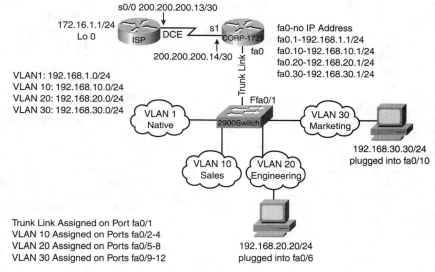

NOTE: This example shows the configuration of the switch only. Part III, "CCNA 3," Chapter 9, "VLAN Trunking Protocol," covers configuration of the routers.

`switch>`**`en`**	Enters privileged mode
`switch#`**`config t`**	Enters global configuration mode
`switch(config)#`**`hostname 2900Switch`**	Sets the host name
`2900Switch(config)#`**`no ip domain-lookup`**	Turns off checking for DNS entries on spelling mistakes
`2900Switch(config)#`**`enable secret cisco`**	Sets the secret password to **cisco**
`2900Switch(config)#`**`line con 0`**	Enters console mode

`2900Switch(config-line)#`**`logging synchronous`**	Informational lines will not affect the command being entered
`2900Switch(config-line)#`**`login`**	Turns on password challenge for console mode
`2900Switch(config-line)#`**`password class`**	Sets password to **class**
`2900Switch(config-line)#`**`exit`**	Returns to global config mode
`2900Switch(config)#`**`line vty 0 15`**	Enters ALL 16 vty modes. The same commands will apply to all lines
`2900Switch(config-line)#`**`login`**	Challenges a remote user for a password
`2900Switch(config-line)#`**`password  class`**	Sets the password to **class**
`2900Switch(config-line)#`**`exit`**	Returns to global config mode
`2900Switch(config)#`**`ip default-gateway 192.168.1.1`**	Sets the default gateway for switch
`2900Switch(config)#`**`int vlan1`**	Enters the virtual interface VLAN 1
`2900Switch(config-if)#`**`ip address 192.168.1.2 255.255.255.0`**	Sets the IP address of the switch
`2900Switch(config-if)#`**`no shut`**	Turns on the interface
`2900Switch(config-if)#`**`exit`**	Returns to global config mode
`2900Switch(config)#`**`exit`**	Returns to privileged mode
`2900Switch#`**`vlan database`**	Enters the VLAN database
`2900Switch(vlan)#`**`vlan 10 name Sales`**	Creates VLAN 10
`2900Switch(vlan)#`**`vlan 20 name Engineering`**	Creates VLAN 20
`2900Switch(vlan)#`**`vlan 30 name Marketing`**	Creates VLAN 30
`2900Switch(vlan)#`**`exit`**	Applies VLAN information and exits
`2900Switch#`**`config t`**	Enters global configuration mode

`2900Switch(config)#int fa0/2`	Moves to interface mode
`2900Switch(config-if)#switchport mode access`	Sets the switchport mode to access
`2900Switch(config-if)#switchport access vlan 10`	Assigns this port to VLAN 10
`2900Switch(config-if)#int fa0/3`	Moves to interface mode
`2900Switch(config-if)#switchport mode access`	Sets the switchport mode to access
`2900Switch(config-if)#switchport access vlan 10`	Assigns this port to VLAN 10
`2900Switch(config)#int fa0/4`	Moves to interface mode
`2900Switch(config-if)#switchport mode access`	Sets the switchport mode to access
`2900Switch(config-if)#switchport access vlan 10`	Assigns this port to VLAN 10
`2900Switch(config-if)#int fa0/5`	Moves to interface mode
`2900Switch(config-if)#switchport mode access`	Sets the switchport mode to access
`2900Switch(config-if)#switchport access vlan 20`	Assigns this port to VLAN 20
`2900Switch(config)#int fa0/6`	Moves to interface mode
`2900Switch(config-if)#switchport mode access`	Sets the switchport mode to access
`2900Switch(config-if)#switchport access vlan 20`	Assigns this port to VLAN 20
`2900Switch(config-if)#int fa0/7`	Moves to interface mode
`2900Switch(config-if)#switchport mode access`	Sets the switchport mode to access
`2900Switch(config-if)#switchport access vlan 20`	Assigns this port to VLAN 20
`2900Switch(config)#int fa0/8`	Moves to interface mode
`2900Switch(config-if)#switchport mode access`	Sets the switchport mode to access
`2900Switch(config-if)#switchport access vlan 20`	Assigns this port to VLAN 20
`2900Switch(config-if)#int fa0/9`	Moves to interface mode

2900Switch(config-if)#**switchport mode access**	Sets the switchport mode to access
2900Switch(config-if)#**switchport access vlan 30**	Assigns this port to VLAN 30
2900Switch(config)#**int fa0/10**	Moves to interface mode
2900Switch(config-if)#**switchport mode access**	Sets the switchport mode to access
2900Switch(config-if)#**switchport access vlan 30**	Assigns this port to VLAN 30
2900Switch(config-if)#**int fa0/11**	Moves to interface mode
2900Switch(config-if)#**switchport mode access**	Sets the switchport mode to access
2900Switch(config-if)#**switchport access vlan 30**	Assigns this port to VLAN 30
2900Switch(config)#**int fa0/12**	Moves to interface mode
2900Switch(config-if)#**switchport mode access**	Sets the switchport mode to access
2900Switch(config-if)#**switchport access vlan 30**	Assigns this port to VLAN 30
2900Switch(config-if)#Ctrl z	Returns to privileged mode
2900Switch#**copy run start**	Saves config to NVRAM

CHAPTER 9

VLAN Trunking Protocol

This chapter provides information and commands concerning the following topics for 1900, 2900, and 2950 series switches:

- Configuring ISL trunks
- Configuring Dot1Q trunks
- Verifying trunking
- VTP configuration
- Confirming VTP configuration
- Inter-VLAN communication: Router-on-a-stick
- Router-on-a-stick tips

Configuring ISL Trunks

NOTE: The 1900 series switch supports only Inter-Switch Link (ISL) trunking. The 2900 series switch supports both ISL and Dot1Q trunking. The 2950 series switch supports only Dot1Q trunking.

1900 Series Switch

1900Switch(config)#**int fa 0/26**	Enters interface mode
1900Switch(config-if)#**trunk on**	Turns trunking mode on

2900 Series Switch

2900Switch(config)#**int fa 0/1**	Enters interface mode
2900Switch(config-if)#**switchport mode trunk**	Turns port to trunking mode
2900Switch(config-if)#**switchport trunk encapsulation isl**	Sets encapsulation type to ISL

NOTE: Trunking can only occur on a Fast Ethernet port. A 1900 series switch has only two Fast Ethernet ports—ports A and B. These are defined as FA 0/26 and FA 0/27 in the command-line interface (CLI).

NOTE: For any series switch, you must set trunk mode at both ends of the link for the trunk to become active

Configuring Dot1Q Trunks

2900 Series Switch

`2900Switch(config)#int fa 0/1`	Enters interface mode
`2900Switch(config-if)#switchport mode trunk`	Turns port to trunking mode
`2900Switch(config-if)#switchport trunk encapsulation dot1q`	Sets encapsulation type to Dot1Q—this is the default encapsulation type

2950 Series Switch

`2950Switch(config)#int fa 0/1`	Enters interface mode
`2950Switch(config-if)#switchport mode trunk`	Turns port to trunking mode

Verifying Trunking

1900 Series Switch

`1900Switch#show trunk A`	Displays trunking information about port 0/26

`DISL state: On, Trunking: On, Encapsulation type: ISL`
 	
`1900Switch#`	

2900 and 2950 Series Switches

`29x0Switch#show int fa 0/1 switchport` Name: Fa0/1 Switchport: Enabled Administrative mode: trunk Operational Mode: trunk Administrative Trunking Encapsulation: isl Operational Trunking Encapsulation: isl <output cut> 29x0Switch#	Shows the status of the interface, including trunking information

VTP Configuration

1900 Series Switch

`1900Switch(config)#`**`vtp client`**	Changes the switch to VTP client mode
`1900Switch(config)#`**`vtp server`**	Changes the switch to default VTP server mode
`1900Switch(config)#`**`vtp transparent`**	Changes the switch to VTP transparent mode
`1900Switch(config)#`**`vtp domain CNAP`**	Sets the name of the VTP management domain to CNAP
`1900Switch(config)#`**`vtp password cisco`**	Sets the VTP password to **cisco**

2900 Series Switch

`2900Switch#`**`vlan database`**	Enters VLAN database mode
`2900Switch(vlan)#`**`vtp client`**	Changes the switch to client mode
`2900Switch(vlan)#`**`vtp server`**	Changes the switch to server mode
`2900Switch(vlan)#`**`vtp transparent`**	Changes the switch to transparent mode
`2900Switch(vlan)#`**`vtp domain academy`**	Sets the name of the VTP management domain to academy
`2900Switch(vlan)#`**`vtp password catalyst`**	Sets the VTP password to **catalyst**
`2900Switch(vlan)#`**`vtp v2-mode`**	Sets VTP mode to version 2
`2900Switch(vlan)#`**`vtp pruning`**	Enables VTP pruning
`2900Switch(vlan)#`**`exit`**	Applies the changes and exits mode
`2900Switch#`	

2950 Series Switch

`2950Switch#`**`config t`**	Enters global config mode
`2950Switch(config)#`**`vtp mode client`**	Changes the switch to client mode
`2950Switch(config)#`**`vtp mode server`**	Changes the switch to server mode

2950Switch(config)#**vtp mode transparent**	Changes the switch to transparent mode
2950Switch(config)#**vtp domain academy**	Sets the name of the VTP management domain to academy
2950Switch(config)#**vtp password catalyst**	Sets the VTP password to catalyst
2950Switch(config)#**vtp v2-mode**	Sets VTP mode to version 2
2950Switch(config)#**vtp pruning**	Enables VTP pruning

NOTE: VTP versions 1 and 2 are not interoperable. All switches must use the same version. The biggest difference between version 1 and 2 is that version 2 has support for Token Ring VLANs.

CAUTION: Switches that are in client mode update their VLAN database from switches that are in server mode. If you have two or more switches interconnected and you delete a VLAN database, you may find that it becomes updated from a server switch because of your VTP mode.

Another serious problem occurs when you take a new switch in server mode (the default mode) and plug it into an existing network. If the VTP revision number is higher on the new switch, it sends an update to all other switches to overwrite their VLAN database with new information—in this case, an empty VLAN database. You now have a production network with no VLAN information.

Recommended practice is that you put a switch into VTP client mode first before adding them into a production network, allow it to receive an update of current VLAN information, and then change it to VTP server mode.

Confirming VTP Configuration

1900 Series Switch

1900Switch#**show vtp**	Displays all VTP information

2900/2950 Series Switch

29x0Switch#**show vtp status**	Displays VTP domain status
29x0Switch#**show vtp counters**	Displays VTP statistics

Inter-VLAN Communication: Router-on-a-Stick

`Router(config)#int fa 0/0`	Enters interface mode for interface FA 0/0
`Router(config-if)#no shut`	Turns the interface on
`Router(config-if)#int fa 0/0.1`	Creates subinterface 0/0.1
`Router(config-subif)#encapsulation dot1q 1 native`	Assigns the native VLAN (usually VLAN 1) to this logical subinterface
`Router(config-subif)#ip address 192.168.1.1 255.255.255.0`	Assigns an IP address to the subinterface
`Router(config-subif)#int fa 0/0.10`	Creates subinterface 0/0.10
`Router(config-subif)#encapsulation dot1q 10`	Assigns VLAN 10 to this subinterface
`Router(config-subif)#ip address 192.168.10.1 255.255.255.0`	Assigns an IP address to the subinterface
`Router(config-subif)#`Ctrl z	
`Router#`	

Router-on-a-Stick Tips

- The 1900 series switch has ISL capability only. If connecting a router to a 1900 series switch, replace the router command **encapsulation dot1q** *x* with **encapsulation isl** *x*.
- The native VLAN (usually VLAN 1) cannot be configured on a logical subinterface in Cisco IOS Software releases earlier than 12.1(3)T. Native IP addresses therefore have to be configured on the physical interface:

```
Router(config)#int fa 0/0
Router(config-if)#encapsulation dot1q 1 native
Router(config-if)#ip address 192.168.1.1 255.255.255.0
Router(config-if)#int fa 0/0.10
Router(config-subif)#encapsulation dot1q 10
Router(config-subif)#ip address 192.168.10.1 255.255.255.0
```

- The 1721 and the 1760 series routers have Dot1Q capability only. They cannot perform ISL encapsulation.
- The 2620 and 2621 series routers have both Dot1Q and ISL encapsulation methods
- The number of the subinterface can be any number from 0–4294967295.
- Use the same number of the VLAN number for the subinterface number. Troubleshooting VLAN 10 on subinterface FA 0/0.10 is more intuitive than troubleshooting it on FA 0/0.2
- On a 1721 or 1760 series router, the name of the Fast Ethernet interface is FA 0.x
- On a 2620 or 2621 series router, the name of the Fast Ethernet interface is FA 0/0.x or 0/1.x

Configuration Example: VTP and Inter-VLAN Routing

Figure 9-1 shows the network topology for the configuration of VTP and inter-VLAN routing. There are separate sections on configuring both 2900 and 2950 series switches.

Figure 9-1   Network Topology for VTP and Inter-VLAN Routing Configuration

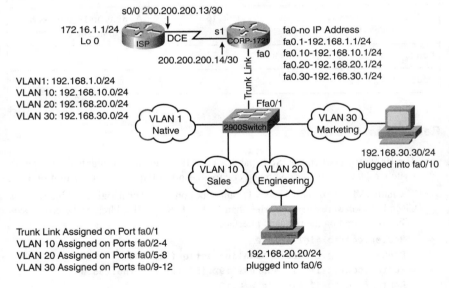

ISP Router

`Router>`**`en`**	
`Router>#`**`config t`**	
`Router(config)#`**`hostname ISP`**	Sets the host name
`ISP(config)#`**`no ip domain-lookup`**	Turns off DNS resolution to avoid wait time due to DNS lookup of spelling errors
`ISP(config)#`**`line con 0`**	
`ISP(config-line)#`**`logging synchronous`**	Appends the command line to a new line—no interruption from info items
`ISP(config-line)#`**`exec-timeout 0 0`**	Console session will never time out
`ISP(config-line)#`**`exit`**	
`ISP(config)#`**`enable secret cisco`**	Sets the secret password to **cisco**
`ISP(config)#`**`int lo 0`**	Creates a loopback address for testing purposes
`ISP(config-if)#`**`description simulated address representing remote website`**	
`ISP(config-if)#`**`ip address 172.16.1.1 255.255.255.0`**	
`ISP(config-if)#`**`int s0/0`**	Enters serial interface configuration mode
`ISP(config-if)#`**`description WAN link to the Corporate Router`**	
`ISP(config-if)#`**`ip address 200.200.200.13 255.255.255.252`**	
`ISP(config-if)#`**`clock 56000`**	Sets the clock rate for the serial link
`ISP(config-if)#`**`no shut`**	

`ISP(config-if)#exit`	
`ISP(config-if)#router eigrp 10`	Turns on the EIGRP routing process
`ISP(config-router)#network 172.16.0.0`	Advertises the 172.16.0.0 network
`ISP(config-router)#network 200.200.200.0`	Advertises the 200.200.200.0 network
`ISP(config-router)#no auto-summary`	Turns off automatic summarization at the classful boundary
`ISP(config-router)#exit`	
`ISP(config)#exit`	
`ISP#copy run start`	Saves the configuration to NVRAM
CORP Router (1721 Router Running Cisco IOS Software Release 12.2(4)	**These Commands Work Also for the 1760 and the 2620/2621 Series Routers**
`Router>en`	
`Router#config t`	
`Router(config)#hostname CORP`	Sets host name
`CORP(config)#no ip domain-lookup`	Turns off resolution to avoid wait time due to DNS lookup of spelling errors
`CORP(config)#line con 0`	
`CORP(config-line)#logging synchronous`	Appends the command line to a new line—no interruption from info items
`CORP(config-line)#exec-timeout 0 0`	Console session will never time out

CORP(config-line)#**exit**	
CORP(config)#**enable secret cisco**	Sets the secret password to **cisco**
CORP(config)#**int s1**	
CORP(config-if)#**desc WAN link to ISP Router**	
CORP(config-if)#**ip add 200.200.200.14 255.255.255.252**	
CORP(config-if)#**no shut**	
CORP(config-if)#**exit**	
CORP(config)#**int fa0**	
CORP(config-if)#**full duplex**	
CORP(config-if)#**no shut**	
CORP(config-if)#**int fa0.1**	Creates a subinterface
CORP(config-subif)#**desc Management VLAN 1**	Assigns a description to the subinterface
CORP(config-subif)#**encapsulation dot1q 1 native**	Enables Dot1Q encapsulation with VLAN 1 as the native VLAN
CORP(config-subif)#**ip add 192.168.1.1 255.255.255.0**	Assigns an IP address to the subinterface
CORP(config-subif)#**int fa0.10**	Creates a subinterface
CORP(config-subif)#**desc Sales VLAN 10**	Assigns a description to the subinterface
CORP(config-subif)#**encapsulation dot1q 10**	Enables Dot1Q encapsulation on VLAN 10
CORP(config-subif)#**ip add 192.168.10.1 255.255.255.0**	Assigns an IP address to the subinterface
CORP(config-subif)#**int fa0.20**	Creates a subinterface

`CORP(config-subif)#desc Engineering VLAN 20`	Assigns a description to the subinterface
`CORP(config-subif)#encapsulation dot1q 20`	Enables Dot1Q encapsulation on VLAN 20
`CORP(config-subif)#ip add 192.168.20.1 255.255.255.0`	Assigns an IP address to the subinterface
`CORP(config-subif)#int fa0.30`	Creates a subinterface
`CORP(config-subif)#desc Marketing VLAN 30`	Assigns a description to the subinterface
`CORP(config-subif)#encapsulation dot1q 30`	Enables Dot1Q encapsulation on VLAN 30
`CORP(config-subif)#ip add 192.168.1.1 255.255.255.0`	Assigns an IP address to the subinterface
`CORP(config-subif)#exit`	
`CORP(config)#router eigrp 10`	Turns on the EIGRP routing process
`CORP(config-router)#network 192.168.1.0`	Advertises the 192.168.1.0 network
`CORP(config-router)#network 192.168.10.0`	Advertises the 192.168.10.0 network
`CORP(config-router)#network 192.168.20.0`	Advertises the 192.168.20.0 network
`CORP(config-router)#network 192.168.30.0`	Advertises the 192.168.30.0 network
`CORP(config-router)#network 200.200.200.0`	Advertises the 200.200.200.0 network
`CORP(config-router)#no auto-summary`	Turns off auto summarization
`CORP(config-router)#exit`	
`CORP(config)#exit`	

CORP#**copy run start**	Saves the configuration to NVRAM
	Caution: Remember to advertise *all* networks. Advertising 192.168.0.0 does not advertise networks from 192.168.0.0– 192.168.255.0. These are separate classful networks, so they must be advertised separately, just like 200.200.200.0 is advertised separately

2900 Series Switch

switch>**en**	
switch>#**config t**	
switch(config)#**hostname 2900Switch**	Sets host name
2900Switch(config)#**no ip domain-lookup**	Turns off DNS resolution to avoid wait time due to DNS lookup of spelling errors
2900Switch(config)#**line con 0**	
2900Switch(config-line)#**logging synchronous**	Appends the command line to a new line—no interruption from info items
2900Switch(config-line)#**exec-timeout 0 0**	Console session will never time out
2900Switch(config-line)#**exit**	
2900Switch(config)#**enable secret cisco**	Sets the secret password to **cisco**
2900Switch(config)#**exit**	
2900Switch#**vlan database**	Enters VLAN database mode

`2900Switch(vlan)#vlan 10 name Sales`	Creates VLAN 10 with the name Sales
`2900Switch(vlan)#vlan 20 name Engineering`	Creates VLAN 20 with the name Engineering
`2900Switch(vlan)#vlan 30 name Marketing`	Creates VLAN 30 with the name Marketing
`2900Switch(vlan)#vtp server`	Makes the switch a VTP server
`2900Switch(vlan)#vtp domain academy`	Assigns a domain name of academy
`2900Switch(vlan)#exit`	Applies all changes to VLAN database and exits mode
`2900Switch#config t`	
`2900Switch(config)#int vlan1`	
`2900Switch(config-if)#ip add 192.168.1.2 255.255.255.0`	
`2900Switch(config-if)#no shutdown`	
`2900Switch(config-if)#exit`	
`2900Switch(config)#ip default-gateway 192.168.1.1`	
`2900Switch(config)#int fa 0/1`	
`2900Switch(config-if)#desc Trunk Link to CORP Router`	
`2900Switch(config-if)#switchport mode trunk`	Creates a trunk link
`2900Switch(config-if)#switchport trunk encapsulation dot1q`	Sets encapsulation to Dot1Q
`2900Switch(config-if)#int fa 0/2`	
`2900Switch(config-if)#switchport access vlan 10`	Assigns a port to VLAN 10

2900Switch(config-if)#**spanning-tree portfast**	Transitions the port directly to the Forwarding state in Spanning Tree Protocol (STP)
	Note: The command **switchport mode access** is not needed, because this is the default mode for interfaces. Use it only if the port was previously set to be a trunk link
2900Switch(config-if)#**int fa0/3**	
2900Switch(config-if)#**switchport access vlan 10**	Assigns a port to VLAN 10
2900Switch(config-if)#**spanning-tree portfast**	Transitions the port directly to the Forwarding state in STP
2900Switch(config-if)#**int fa0/4**	
2900Switch(config-if)#**switchport access vlan 10**	Assigns a port to VLAN 10
2900Switch(config-if)#**spanning-tree portfast**	Transitions the port directly to the Forwarding state in STP
2900Switch(config-if)#**int fa0/5**	
2900Switch(config-if)#**switchport access vlan 20**	Assigns a port to VLAN 20
2900Switch(config-if)#**spanning-tree portfast**	Transitions the port directly to the Forwarding state in STP
2900Switch(config-if)#**int fa0/6**	
2900Switch(config-if)#**switchport access vlan 20**	Assigns a port to VLAN 20
2900Switch(config-if)#**spanning-tree portfast**	Transitions the port directly to the Forwarding state in STP
2900Switch(config-if)#**int fa0/7**	
2900Switch(config-if)#**switchport access vlan 20**	Assigns a port to VLAN 20

`2900Switch(config-if)#spanning-tree portfast`	Transitions the port directly to the Forwarding state in STP
`2900Switch(config-if)#int fa0/8`	
`2900Switch(config-if)#switchport access vlan 20`	Assigns a port to VLAN 20
`2900Switch(config-if)#spanning-tree portfast`	Transitions the port directly to the Forwarding state in STP
`2900Switch(config-if)#int fa0/9`	
`2900Switch(config-if)#switchport access vlan 30`	Assigns a port to VLAN 30
`2900Switch(config-if)#spanning-tree portfast`	Transitions the port directly to the Forwarding state in STP
`2900Switch(config-if)#int fa0/10`	
`2900Switch(config-if)#switchport access vlan 30`	Assigns a port to VLAN 30
`2900Switch(config-if)#spanning-tree portfast`	Transitions the port directly to the Forwarding state in STP
`2900Switch(config-if)#int fa0/11`	
`2900Switch(config-if)#switchport access vlan 30`	Assigns a port to VLAN 30
`2900Switch(config-if)#spanning-tree portfast`	Transitions the port directly to the Forwarding state in STP
`2900Switch(config-if)#int fa0/12`	
`2900Switch(config-if)#switchport access vlan 30`	Assigns a port to VLAN 30
`2900Switch(config-if)#spanning-tree portfast`	Transitions the port directly to the Forwarding state in STP
`2900Switch(config-if)#`Ctrl Z	
`2900Switch#copy run start`	Saves the configuration to NVRAM
`2900Switch#`	

2950 Series Switch

switch>**en**	
switch>#**config t**	
switch(config)#**hostname 2950Switch**	Sets the host name
2950Switch(config)#**no ip domain-lookup**	Turns off DNS resolution to avoid wait time due to DNS lookup of spelling errors
2950Switch(config)#**line con 0**	
2950Switch(config-line)#**logging synchronous**	Appends the command line to a new line—no interruption from info items
2950Switch(config-line)#**exec-timeout 0 0**	Console session will never time out
2950Switch(config-line)#**exit**	
2950Switch(config)#**enable secret cisco**	Sets the secret password to **cisco**
2950Switch(config)#**vlan 10**	Creates VLAN 10
2950Switch(config-vlan)#**name Sales**	Defines the name of Sales
2950Switch(config-vlan)#**vlan 20**	Creates VLAN 20
2950Switch(config-vlan)#**name Engineering**	Defines the name of Engineering
2950Switch(config-vlan)#**vlan 30**	Creates VLAN 30
2950Switch(config-vlan)#**name Marketing**	Defines the name of Marketing
2950Switch(config-vlan)#**exit**	
2950Switch(config)#**vtp mode server**	Makes the switch a VTP server
2950Switch(config)#**vtp domain academy**	Assigns a domain name of academy

`2950Switch(config)#int vlan1`	Creates the virtual VLAN 1 interface
`2950Switch(config-if)#ip add 192.168.1.2 255.255.255.0`	Assigns an IP address to the interface
`2950Switch(config-if)#no shutdown`	
`2950Switch(config-if)#exit`	
`2950Switch(config)#ip default-gateway 192.168.1.1`	Assigns the IP address of the default gateway
`2950Switch(config)#int fa 0/1`	
`2950Switch(config-if)#desc Trunk Link to CORP Router`	
`2950Switch(config-if)#switchport mode trunk`	Creates a trunk link
`2950Switch(config-if)#int range fa 0/2 - 4`	
`2950Switch(config-if-range)#switchport access vlan 10`	Assigns ports to VLAN 10
`2950Switch(config-if-range)#spanning-tree portfast`	Transitions ports directly to the Forwarding state in STP
	Note: The command **switchport mode access** is not needed, because this is the default mode for interfaces. Use it only if the port was previously set to be a trunk link
`2950Switch(config-if-range)#int range fa0/5 - 8`	
`2950Switch(config-if-range)#switchport access vlan 20`	Assigns ports to VLAN 20
`2950Switch(config-if-range)#spanning-tree portfast`	Transitions ports directly to the Forwarding state in STP
`2950Switch(config-if-range)#int range fa0/9 - 12`	

2950Switch(config-if-range)#**switchport access vlan 30**	Assigns ports to VLAN 10
2950Switch(config-if-range)#**spanning-tree portfast**	Transitions ports directly to the Forwarding state in STP
2950Switch(config-if-range)#**Ctrl z**	
2950Switch#**copy run start**	Saves the configuration to NVRAM

CHAPTER 1

Scaling IP Technologies

This chapter provides information and commands concerning the following topics:

- Configuring dynamic NAT
- Configuring PAT
- Configuring static NAT
- Verifying NAT and PAT configuration
- Troubleshooting NAT and PAT configuration
- Configuring DHCP
- Verifying and troubleshooting DHCP configuration
- Configuring a DHCP helper address

The following table lists the address ranges as specified in RFC 1918 that can be used as internal private addresses. These will be your "inside the LAN" addresses that will have to be translated into public addresses that can be routed across the Internet. Any network is allowed to use these addresses; however, these addresses are not allowed to be routed onto the public Internet.

Private Addresses		
Class	**RFC 1918 Internal Address Range**	**CIDR Prefix**
A	10.0.0.0–10.255.255.255	10.0.0.0/8
B	172.16.0.0–172.31.255.255	172.16.0.0/12
C	192.168.0.0–192.168.255.255	192.168.0.0/16

Configuring Dynamic NAT: One Private to One Public Address Translation

> **NOTE:** For a complete configuration of NAT/PAT with a diagram for visual assistance, see the sample configuration at the end of this chapter

Step 1: Define a static route on the remote router stating where public addresses should be routed.	ISP(config)#ip route 64.64.64.64 255.255.255.128 s0/0	Informs the ISP router where to send packets with addresses destined for 64.64.64.64 255.255.255.255.128
Step 2: Define a pool of usable public IP addresses on your router that will perform NAT.		Private address will receive first available public address in pool
	Corp(config)#ip nat pool scott 64.64.64.70 64.64.64.126 netmask 255.255.255.128	Defines the following: • Name of pool is **scott** (the name of the pool can be anything) • Start of pool is **64.64.64.70** • End of pool is **64.64.64.126** • Subnet mask is **255.255.255.128**
Step 3: Create an ACL that will identify which private IP addresses will be translated.	Corp(config)#access-list 1 permit 172.16.10.0 0.0.0.255	
Step 4: Link the access control list (ACL) to the pool of addresses (create the translation).	Corp(config)#ip nat inside source list 1 pool scott	Defines the following: • The source of the private addresses is from ACL 1 • The pool of available public addresses is named **scott**
Step 5: Define which interfaces are inside (contain the private addresses).	Router(config)#int fa 0/0	
	Router(config-if)#ip nat inside	You can have more than one inside interface on a router. Addresses from each inside interface are then allowed to be translated into a public address

Step 6: Define the outside interface (the interface leading to the public network).	`Router(config)#int s 0/0`	
	`Router(config-if)#ip nat outside`	

Configuring PAT: Many Private to One Public Address Translation

Private addresses all use a single public IP address and numerous port numbers for translation.

Step 1: Define a static route on the remote router stating where public addresses should be routed.	`ISP(config)#ip route`
	`64.64.64.64 255.255.255.128`
	`s0/0`
		Informs the ISP where to send packets with addresses destined for 64.64.64.64 255.255.255.128

Step 2: Define a pool of usable public IP addresses on your router that will perform NAT (optional).		Use this step if you have many private addresses to translate. A single public IP address can handle thousands of private addresses. Without using a pool of addresses, you can translate all private addresses into the IP address of the exit interface—the serial link to the ISP, for example

	`Corp(config)#ip nat pool`
	`scott 64.64.64.70`
	`64.64.64.126 netmask`
	`255.255.255.128`
		Defines the following:
		• Name of pool is **scott** (the name of the pool can be anything)
		• Start of pool is **64.64.64.70**
		• End of pool is **64.64.64.126**
		• Subnet mask is **255.255.255.128**

Step 3: Create an ACL that will identify which private IP addresses will be translated.	`Corp(config)#access-list 1 permit 172.16.10.0 0.0.0.255`	
Step 4 (Option 1): Link the ACL to the outside public interface (create the translation).	`Corp(config)#ip nat inside source list 1 interface serial 0/0 overload`	The source of the private addresses is from ACL 1 The public address to be translated into is the one assigned to Serial 0/0 The **overload** keyword states that port numbers will be used to handle many translations
Step 4 (Option 2): Link the ACL to the pool of addresses (create the translation).		If using the pool created in Step 1
	`Corp(config)#ip nat inside source list 1 pool scott overload`	The source of the private addresses is from ACL 1 The pool of available addresses is named **scott** The **overload** keyword states that port numbers will be used to handle many translations
Step 5: Define which interfaces are inside (contain the private addresses).	`Corp(config)#int fa 0/0`	
	`Corp(config-if)#ip nat inside`	You can have more than one inside interface on a router
Step 6: Define the outside interface (the interface leading to the public network).	`Corp(config)#int s 0/0`	
	`Corp(config-if)#ip nat outside`	

Configuring Static NAT: One Private to One Permanent Public Address Translation

Step 1: Define a static route on the remote router stating where public addresses should be routed.	`ISP(config)#ip route 64.64.64.64 255.255.255.128 s0/0`	Informs the ISP where to send packets with addresses destined for 64.64.64.64 255.255.255.128
Step 2: Create a static mapping on your router that will perform NAT.	`Corp(config)ip nat inside source static 172.16.10.5 64.64.64.65`	Permanently translates inside address of 172.16.10.5 to a public address of 64.64.64.65 Use the command for each of the private IP addresses you want to statically map to a public address
Step 3: Define which interfaces are inside (contain the private addresses).	`Corp(config)#int fa 0/0`	
	`Corp(config-if)#ip nat inside`	You can have more than one inside interface on a router
Step 4: Define the outside interface (the interface leading to the public network).	`Corp(config)#int s 0/0`	
	`Corp(config-if)#ip nat outside`	

CAUTION: Make sure that you have in your router configurations a way for packets to travel back to your NAT router. Include a static route on the ISP router advertising your NAT pool and how to travel back to your internal network. Without this in place, a packet can leave your network with a public address, but will not be able to return if your ISP router does not know where the pool of public addresses exists in the network. You should be advertising the pool of public addresses, not your private addresses.

Verifying NAT and PAT Configuration

Router#**show ip nat translations**	Displays translation table
Router#**show ip nat statistics**	Displays NAT statistics
Router#**clear ip nat translations inside** *a.b.c.d* **outside** *e.f.g.h*	Clears a specific translation from the table before they time out
Router#**clear ip nat translations ***	Clears the entire translation table before entries time out

Troubleshooting NAT and PAT Configuration

Router#**debug ip nat**	Displays information about every packet that is translated Be careful with this command. The router's CPU might not be able to handle this amount of output and might therefore hang the system
Router#**debug ip nat detailed**	Displays greater detail about packets being translated

Configuring DHCP

Router(config)#**ip dhcp pool academy**	Creates a DHCP pool called academy
Router(dhcp-config)#**network 172.16.10.0 255.255.255.0**	Defines the range of addresses to be leased
Router(dhcp-config)#**default-router 172.16.10.1**	Defines the address of the default router for the client
Router(dhcp-config)#**dns-server 172.16.10.10**	Defines the address of the DNS server for the client
Router(dhcp-config)#**netbios-name-server 172.16.10.10**	Defines the address of the NetBIOS server for the client

`Router(dhcp-config)#domain-name empson.ca`	Defines the domain name for the client
`Router(dhcp-config)#lease 14 12 23`	Defines the lease time to be 14 days, 12 hours, 23 minutes
`Router(dhcp-config)#lease infinite`	Sets the lease time to infinity (default time is 1 day)
`Router(dhcp-config)#exit`	
`Router(config)#ip dhcp excluded-address 172.16.10.1 172.16.10.9`	Specifies the range of addresses not to be leased out to clients
`Router(config)#no service dhcp`	Turns the DHCP service off (service is on by default in IOS)
`Router(config)#service dhcp`	Turns the DHCP service on

Verifying and Troubleshooting DHCP Configuration

`Router#show ip dhcp binding`	Displays a list of all bindings created
`Router#show ip dhcp server statistics`	Displays a list of the number of messages sent and received by the DHCP server
`Router#debug ip dhcp server events`	Displays the DHCP process of addresses being leased and returned

Configuring a DHCP Helper Address

`Router(config)#int fa 0/0`	
`Router(config-if)#ip helper-address 172.16.20.2`	Defines that DHCP broadcasts will be forwarded to this specific address rather than be dropped by the router

Configuration Example: Port Address Translation

Figure 1-1 shows the network topology for the PAT configuration that follows using the commands covered in this chapter.

Figure 1-1   Port Address Translation Configuration

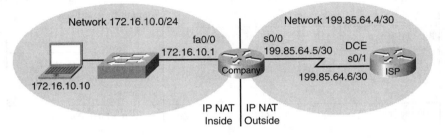

ISP Router

`router>en`	
`router#config t`	
`router(config)#host ISP`	Sets host name
`ISP(config)#no ip domain-lookup`	Turns off DNS resolution to avoid wait time due to DNS lookup of spelling errors
`ISP(config)#enable secret cisco`	Sets encrypted password
`ISP(config)#line con 0`	
`ISP(config-line)#login`	
`ISP(config-line)#password class`	Sets console line password to **class**
`ISP(config-line)#logging synchronous`	Commands will be appended to a new line
`ISP(config-line)#exit`	
`ISP(config)#int s 0/1`	
`ISP(config-if)#ip address 199.85.64.6 255.255.255.252`	Assigns IP address

`ISP(config-if)#clockrate 56000`	Assigns clock rate to data commu-nications equipment (DCE) cable on this side of link
`ISP(config-if)#no shut`	
`ISP(config-if)#int lo0`	Creates loopback interface 0
`ISP(config-if)#ip address 200.200.200.1 255.255.255.255`	Assigns IP address
`ISP(config-if)#exit`	
`ISP(config)#exit`	
`ISP#copy run start`	Saves config to NVRAM

Company Router

`router>en`	
`router#config t`	
`router(config)#host Company`	Sets host name
`Company(config)#no ip domain-lookup`	Turns off DNS resolution to avoid wait time due to DNS lookup of spelling errors
`Company(config)#enable secret cisco`	Sets secret password
`Company(config)#line con 0`	
`Company(config-line)#login`	
`Company(config-line)#password class`	Sets console line password to class
`Company(config-line)#logging synchronous`	Commands will be appended to a new line
`Company(config-line)#exit`	
`Company(config)#int fa 0/0`	
`Company(config-if)#ip address 172.16.10.1 255.255.255.0`	
`Company(config-if)#no shut`	
`Company(config-if)#int s0/0`	

`Company(config-if)#ip add 199.85.64.5 255.255.255.252`	
`Company(config-if)#no shut`	
`Company(config-if)#exit`	
`Company(config)#ip route 0.0.0.0 0.0.0.0 199.85.64.6`	Sends all packets not defined in the routing table to the ISP router
`Company(config)#access-list 1 permit 172.16.10.0 0.0.0.255`	Defines which addresses are permitted through—these addresses are those that will be allowed to be translated with NAT
`Company(config)#ip nat inside source list 1 int s 0/0 overload`	Creates NAT by combining List 1 with the interface S0/0. Overloading will take place
`Company(config)#int fa 0/0`	
`Company(config-if)#ip nat inside`	Location of private inside addresses
`Company(config-if)#int s 0/0`	
`Company(config-if)#ip nat outside`	Location of public outside addresses
`Company(config-if)#`Ctrl z	
`Company#copy run start`	

CHAPTER 2

WAN Technologies

There are no commands affiliated with this module of CCNA 4 as covered in the Cisco Networking Academy Program curriculum.

CHAPTER 3

PPP

This chapter provides information and commands concerning the following Point-to-Point Protocol (PPP) topics:

- Configuring High-Level Data Link Control (HDLC) encapsulation on a serial line
- Configuring PPP on a serial line (mandatory commands)
- Configuring PPP on a serial line (optional commands), including those commands concerning the following:
  — Compression
  — Link quality
  — Multilink
  — Authentication
- Verifying or troubleshooting a serial link/PPP encapsulation

Configuring HDLC Encapsulation on a Serial Line

Router#**config t**	
Router(config)#**int s 0/0**	
Router(config-if))#**encapsulation hdlc**	

NOTE: HDLC is the default encapsulation for synchronous serial links on Cisco routers. You would only use the **encapsulation hdlc** command to return the link back to its default state.

Configuring PPP on a Serial Line (Mandatory Commands)

Router#**config t**	
Router(config)#**int s 0/0**	
Router(config-if) #**encapsulation ppp**	Changes encapsulation from default HDLC to PPP

NOTE: You must execute the **encapsulation ppp** command on both sides of the serial link for the link to become active.

Configuring PPP on a Serial Line (Optional Commands): Compression

`Router(config-if)#compress predictor`	Enables the predictor compression algorithm
`Router(config-if)#compress stac`	Enables the stac compression algorithm

Configuring PPP on a Serial Line (Optional Commands): Link Quality

`Router(config-if)#ppp quality x`	Ensures the link must have a quality of x percent; otherwise, the link will shut down

NOTE: In PPP, the Link Control Protocol allows for an optional link quality determination phase. In this phase, the link is tested to determine whether the link quality is sufficient to bring up any Layer 3 protocols. If you use the command **ppp quality** x, where x is equal to a certain percent, you must meet that percentage of quality on the link. If the link does not meet that percentage level, the link cannot be created and will shut down.

Configuring PPP on a Serial Line (Optional Commands): Multilink

`Router(config-if)#ppp multilink`	Enables load balancing across multiple links

Configuring PPP on a Serial Line (Optional Commands): Authentication

`Router(config)#username routerb password cisco`	Sets a username of **routerb** and a password of **cisco** for authentication from the other side of the PPP serial link. This is used by the local router to authenticate the PPP peer
`Router(config)#int s 0/0`	

`Router(config-if)#`**`ppp authentication pap`**	Turns on PAP authentication only
`Router(config-if)#`**`ppp authentication chap`**	Turns on CHAP authentication only
`Router(config-if)#`**`ppp authentication pap chap`**	Defines that the link will use PAP authentication, but will try CHAP if PAP fails or is rejected by other side
`Router(config-if)#`**`ppp authentication chap pap`**	Defines that the link will use CHAP authentication, but will try PAP if CHAP fails or is rejected by other side
`Router(config-if)#`**`ppp pap sent-username routerb password cisco`**	This command must be set if using PAP in Cisco IOS Software Release 11.1 or later

TIP: When setting authentication, make sure that your usernames match the name of the router on the other side of the link, and that the passwords on each router match each other. Usernames and passwords are case-sensitive. Consider the following example:

`Edmonton(config)#`**`username Calgary password cisco`**	`Calgary(config)#`**`username Edmonton password cisco`**
`Edmonton(config)#`**`int s 0/0`**	`Calgary(config)#`**`int s 0/0`**
`Edmonton(config-if)#`**`encapsulation ppp`**	`Calgary(config-if)#`**`encapsulation ppp`**
`Edmonton(config-if)#`**`ppp authentication chap`**	`Calgary(config-if)#`**`ppp authentication chap`**

NOTE: Because Password Authentication Protocol (PAP) does not encrypt its password as it is sent across the link, recommended practice is that you use Challenge Handshake Authentication Protocol (CHAP) as your authentication method.

Verifying or Troubleshooting a Serial Link/PPP Encapsulation

`Router#show interfaces serial x`	Lists info for serial interface *x*
`Router#show controllers serial x`	Tells you what type of cable (DCE/DTE) is plugged into your interface and whether a clock rate has been set
`Router#debug serial interface`	Displays whether serial keepalive counters are incrementing
`Router#debug ppp`	Displays any traffic related to PPP
`Router#debug ppp packet`	Displays PPP packets that are being sent and received
`Router#debug ppp negotiation`	Displays PPP packets related to the negotiation of the PPP link
`Router#debug ppp error`	Displays PPP error packets
`Router#debug ppp authentication`	Displays PPP packets related to the authentication of the PPP link
`Router#debug ppp compression`	Displays PPP packets related to the compression of packets across the link

TIP: With frequent lab use, serial cable pins often get bent, which may prevent the router from seeing the cable. The output from the command **show controllers interface serial** *x* will show **no cable** even though a cable is physically present.

Configuration Example: PPP

Figure 3-1 shows the network topology for the configuration that follows, which shows how to configure PPP using the commands covered in this chapter.

Figure 3-1   *Network Topology for PPP Configuration*

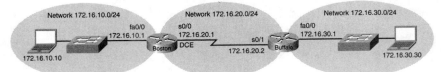

NOTE: The host name, password, and interfaces have all been configured as per
the configuration example in Part II, "CCNA 2," Chapter 3, "Configuring a Router."

Boston Router

Boston>en	
Boston#config t	
Boston(config)#username Buffalo password academy	Sets the local username and password for PPP authentication of the PPP peer
Boston(config-if)#int s 0/0	
Boston(config-if)#desc Link to Buffalo Router	Defines the locally significant link description
Boston(config-if)#ip add 172.16.20.1 255.255.255.0	Assigns IP address to interface
Boston(config-if)#clockrate 56000	Sets clock rate to data communications equipment (DCE) side of link
Boston(config-if) #encapsulation ppp	Turns on PPP encapsulation
Boston(config-if)#ppp authentication chap	Turns on CHAP authentication
Boston(config-if)#no shut	Turns on interface
Boston(config-if)#exit	Exits interface mode
Boston(config)#exit	Exits global config mode
Boston#copy run start	Saves config to NVRAM

Buffalo Router

Buffalo>en	
Buffalo#config t	
Buffalo(config)#username Boston password academy	Sets username and password for PPP authentication
Buffalo(config-if)#int s 0/1	

`Buffalo(config-if)#`**`desc Link to Boston`** **`Router`**	Defines the locally significant link description
`Buffalo(config-if)#`**`ip add 172.16.20.2`** **`255.255.255.0`**	Assigns IP address to interface
`Buffalo(config-if)` **`#encapsulation ppp`**	Turns on PPP encapsulation
`Buffalo(config-if)#`**`ppp authentication`** **`chap`**	Turns on CHAP authentication
`Buffalo(config-if)#`**`no shut`**	Turns on interface
`Buffalo(config-if)#`Ctrl z	Exits back to privileged mode
`Buffalo#`**`copy run start`**	Saves config to NVRAM

CHAPTER 4

ISDN and DDR

This chapter provides information and commands concerning the following topics:

- Setting the switch type in an Integrated Services Digital Network (ISDN) Basic Rate Interface (BRI) configuration
- Setting service profile identifiers (SPIDs) in an ISDN BRI configuration
- Configuring ISDN Primary Rate Interface (PRI)
- Verifying ISDN configuration
- Troubleshooting ISDN
- Configuring legacy dial-on-demand routing (DDR)
- Configuring dialer profiles with DDR

Configuring ISDN BRI: Setting the Switch Type

`Router(config)#`**`isdn switch-type`** *`switch-type`*	Sets the switch type globally for all ISDN interfaces
`Router(config)#`**`int bri 0`**	
`Router(config-ifg)#`**`isdn switch-type`** *`switch-type`*	Sets the switch type for this specific interface. Can be different from global switch type if necessary

NOTE: The switch type will be given to you from your service provider.

A main office with 30 branch offices might have 28 offices using one switch type and two offices using a different switch type. Thus, you would use the global-level command to set the switch type to the one required by the 28 offices, and the interface-level command to override this on the two interfaces that needed a different switch type.

Configuring ISDN BRI: Setting SPIDs

Router(config)#**interface bri 0**	
Router(config-if)#**isdn spid1** **51055510000001 5551000**	Defines the SPID number for channel B1, as assigned by the service provider The second number (5551000) is the local dial directory number (LDN), which usually matches the information coming from the ISDN switch
Router(config-if)#**isdn spid2** **51055510010001 5551001**	Defines the SPID number for channel B2, as assigned by the service provider

NOTE: Not all switch types need SPIDs assigned to your router. Your service provider will let you know whether you need to configure SPIDs.

Configuring ISDN PRI

Router(config)#**isdn switch-type** *switch-type*	Same command as with BRI. Can be done globally or in interface config mode
Router(config)#**controller t1 1/0**	Enters into controller config mode where the PRI card is located
Router(config-controller)#**framing** **{sf ¦ esf}**	Sets framing to either Superframe Format (SF) or Extended Superframe Format (ESF) as dictated by the service provider. ESF is the most commonly used framing
Router(config-controller)#**linecode** **{ami ¦ b8zs ¦ hdb3}**	Sets Layer 1 signaling method to alternate mark inversion (AMI), binary 8-zero substitution (B8ZS) or high-density bipolar three (HDB3). B8ZS is used in North America
Router(config-controller)#**pri-group** **timeslots 1-24**	Configures the number of timeslots allocated by the provider, if using a channelized T1 controller
Router(config-controller)#**interface** **serial0/0:23**	Specifies an interface to be used for PRI D-channel operation. This command says to use channel 24 of interface Serial 0/0

NOTE: Channels are numbered starting at zero (0) not one (1). Therefore, the 16th channel would be numbered 15; channel 24 would be numbered 23.

CAUTION: Subinterfaces on a serial interface are shown with a dot (.). Channels are shown with a colon (:). For example,

Serial0/0.23 is subinterface 23.

Serial 0/0:23 is channel 23.

Verifying ISDN Configuration

Router#`show isdn status`	Confirms BRI operations
Router#`show isdn active`	Displays current call information
Router#`show dialer`	Displays information about the dialer interface (used in DDR)
Router#`show interface bri 0/0`	Displays statistics about interface bri 0/0
Router#`show interface bri 0/0:1`	Displays statistics about channel 1 of interface bri 0/0
Rourer#`clear interface bri 0/0`	Manually resets the interface. All ISDN information will have to be re-sent

TIP: If, after you have set the SPIDs on an interface, the SPIDs have not been sent and verified by the ISDN switch, issue a **clear interface bri 0/0** (or **bri 0**) command to force the router to renegotiate ISDN info with the switch. You might need to issue the **clear interface command** three or four times for the interface to come up.

Troubleshooting ISDN

Router#`debug isdn q921`	Displays info about Layer 2 (data link layer) access taking place on the D channel
Router#`debug isdn q931`	Displays info about Layer 3 (network layer) call setup and teardown between your router and the service provider switch
Router#`debug dialer events`	Displays messages when the DDR link has connected and what traffic caused it to connect
Router#`debug dialer packets`	Displays a message every time a packet is sent out the DDR interface

> **NOTE:** PPP is often used as an encapsulation method when working with ISDN. Therefore, the PPP configuration commands, along with the PPP **debug** commands are applicable here, too.

Configuring Legacy DDR

Step 1: Configure static routes on router.		Using static routes instead of dynamic routing will save on ISDN costs. The link will not always be up because routing updates trigger link to become active
	Edmonton#`config t`	
	Edmonton(config)#`ip route 172.16.30.0 0.0.0.255 172.16.20.2`	
Step 2 (Option 1): Define interesting traffic without access lists.		Specifies what type of traffic will trigger the router to make an ISDN call to establish the link **Tip:** The **dialer-list** and **dialer-group** commands can be compared to the **access-list** and **access-group** commands in access control lists (ACLs)
	Edmonton(config)#`dialer-list 1 protocol ip permit`	States that all IP traffic is interesting
	Edmonton(config)#`int bri 0`	
	Edmonton(config-if)#`dialer-group 1`	Groups all **dialer-list 1** statements together to apply to this interface
Step 2 (Option 2): Define interesting traffic with access lists (for better control).		Using access lists within dialer lists gives you more control as to what traffic is defined as interesting
	Edmonton(config)#`dialer-list 2 protocol ip list 150`	Points dialer list to ACL 150
	Edmonton(config)#`access-list 150 deny udp any any eq tftp`	Denies TFTP traffic

	Edmonton(config)#**access-list 150 deny tcp any any eq telnet**	Denies Telnet traffic
	Edmonton(config)#**access-list 150 permit ip any any**	Permits everything else
	Edmonton(config)#**int bri 0**	
	Edmonton(config-if)#**dialer-group 2**	Groups all **dialer-list 2** statements together on this interface
Step 3: Configure DDR dialer information.		
	Edmonton(config)#**username Calgary password academy**	For PPP encapsulation with authentication across ISDN (optional)
	Edmonton(config)#**int bri 0**	
	Edmonton(config-if)#**encap ppp**	Turns on PPP encapsulation
	Edmonton(config-if)#**ppp authentication chap**	Turns on CHAP authentication
	Edmonton(config-if)#**dialer idle-timeout 150**	Specifies the number of seconds after last interesting traffic is sent before the call terminates(default is 120 seconds)
	Edmonton(config-if)#**dialer map ip 172.16.20.2 name Calgary 5552000**	Defines the following: • 172.16.20.2 = IP address of next-hop router • Calgary = host name of remote router • 5552000 = number to dial to get there

Configuring Dialer Profiles with DDR

TIP: Using a dial map applies the configuration directly to the interface. Using a dialer profile allows you to have a more dynamic configuration—the physical interface will act differently depending on your specific call requirements, such as the following:

• Do you want HDLC encapsulation instead of PPP?

• Do you want an extended ACL rather than a standard one?

• Do you want a different idle-timeout threshold?

Step 1: Configure static routes on router.		Using static routes rather than dynamic routing will save on ISDN costs. The link will not always be up because routing updates trigger link to remain become active
	`Edmonton#config t`	
	`Edmonton(config)#ip route` `172.16.30.0 0.0.0.255 172.16.20.2`	
Step 2 (Option 1): Define interesting traffic without access lists.		
	`Edmonton(config)#dialer-list 1` `protocol ip permit`	
	`Edmonton(config)#int dialer 0`	Go to virtual dialer interface as opposed to physical BRI 0 interface
	`Edmonton(config-if)#dialer-group 1`	
Step 2 (Option 2): Define interesting traffic with access lists.		
	`Edmonton(config)#dialer-list 2` `protocol ip list 150`	
	`Edmonton(config)#access-list 150` `deny udp any any eq tftp`	
	`Edmonton(config)#access-list 150` `deny tcp any any eq telnet`	
	`Edmonton(config)#access-list 150` `permit ip any any`	
	`Edmonton(config)#int dialer 0`	Go to virtual dialer interface as opposed to physical BRI 0 interface.
	`Edmonton(config-if)#dialer-group 2`	

Step 3: Configure DDR dialer information.		
	`Edmonton(config)#username Calgary password academy`	For PPP encapsulation across ISDN (optional)
	`Edmonton(config)#int dialer 0`	
	`Edmonton(config-if)#ip address 172.16.20.1 255.255.255.0`	
	`Edmonton(config-if)#int bri 0`	
	`Edmonton(config-if)#encap ppp`	Turns on PPP encapsulation
	`Edmonton(config-if)#ppp authentication chap`	Turns on CHAP authentication
	`Edmonton(config-if)#dialer idle-timeout 150`	Specifies the number of seconds after last interesting traffic is sent before the call terminates (default is 120 seconds)
Step 4: Configure dialer information.		
	`Edmonton(config)#int dialer 0`	Enters dialer interface
	`Edmonton(config-if)#dialer remote name Calgary`	
	`Edmonton(config-if)#dialer string 5552000`	
Step 5: Associate dialer profile.		
	`Edmonton(config)#interface bri 0`	
	`Edmonton(config-if)#dialer pool-member 1`	Or **2** if using **dial-group 2**
	`Edmonton(config-if)#interface dialer 0`	
	`Edmonton(config-if)#dialer pool 1`	Or **2** if using **dial-group 2**

Configuration Example: ISDN and DDR with No Dialer Profiles

Figure 4-1 shows the network topology for the ISDN and DDR with no dialer profiles configuration that follows using the commands covered in this chapter.

Figure 4-1   ISDN/DDR with No Dialer Profiles Configuration

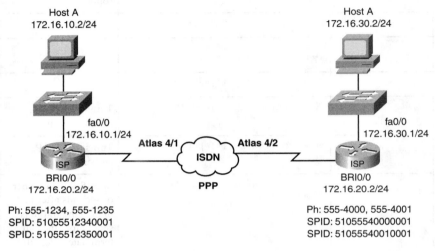

Host A
172.16.10.2/24

Host A
172.16.30.2/24

fa0/0
172.16.10.1/24

fa0/0
172.16.30.1/24

Atlas 4/1   **ISDN**   **Atlas 4/2**

ISP   ISP

BRI0/0
172.16.20.2/24

PPP

BRI0/0
172.16.20.2/24

Ph: 555-1234, 555-1235
SPID: 51055512340001
SPID: 51055512350001

Ph: 555-4000, 555-4001
SPID: 51055540000001
SPID: 51055540010001

Edmonton Router

`router>`**`en`**	
`router#`**`config t`**	
`router(config)#`**`host Edmonton`**	Sets host name
`Edmonton(config)#`**`no ip domain-lookup`**	Turns off DNS resolution to avoid wait time due to DNS lookup of spelling errors
`Edmonton(config)#`**`enable secret cisco`**	Sets encrypted password to **cisco**
`Edmonton(config)#`**`line con 0`**	
`Edmonton(config-line)#`**`login`**	
`Edmonton(config-line)#`**`password class`**	Sets console line password to **class**

Edmonton(config-line)#**logging synchronous**	Returns prompt to same location after info messages interrupt
Edmonton(config-line)#**exit**	
Edmonton(config)#**int fa 0/0**	
Edmonton(config-if)#**ip add 172.16.10.1 255.255.255.0**	Assigns IP address to interface
Edmonton(config-if)#**no shut**	Turns interface on
Edmonton(config-if)#**exit**	
Edmonton(config)#**username Calgary password academy**	For PPP encapsulation across ISDN (optional)
Edmonton(config)#**isdn switch-type basic-ni**	Sets ISDN switch type for all interfaces to match service provider
Edmonton(config)#**dialer-list 1 protocol ip permit**	Defines interesting traffic—all IP
Edmonton(config)#**ip route 0.0.0.0 0.0.0.0 172.16.20.2**	Creates a static route that will send all traffic not defined in the routing table to the next-hop address of 172.16.20.2
Edmonton(config)#**int bri 0/0**	
Edmonton(config-if)#**ip add 172.16.20.1 255.255.255.0**	Assigns IP address to interface
Edmonton(config-if)#**encap ppp**	Turns on PPP encapsulation
Edmonton(config-if)#**ppp authen chap**	Turns on CHAP authentication
Edmonton(config-if)#**dialer-group 1**	Assigns traffic from dialer list 1 to this group
Edmonton(config-if)#**isdn spid1 51055512340001 5551234**	Assigns SPID 1
Edmonton(config-if)#**isdn spid2 51055512350001 5551235**	Assigns SPID 2
Edmonton(config-if)#**dialer idle-timeout 90**	Specifies that the interface will disconnect after 90 seconds of no traffic

Edmonton(config-if)#**dialer map ip 172.16.20.2 name Calgary 5554000**	Sets map to find remote router
Edmonton(config-if)#**no shut**	
Edmonton(config-if)#Ctrl z	
Edmonton#**copy run start**	Saves configuration to NVRAM

Calgary Router

router>**en**	
router#**config t**	
router(config)#**host Calgary**	Sets host name
Calgary(config)#**no ip domain-lookup**	Turns off DNS resolution to avoid wait time due to DNS lookup of spelling errors
Calgary(config)#**enable secret cisco**	Sets encrypted password
Calgary(config)#**line con 0**	
Calgary(config-line)#**login**	
Calgary(config-line)#**password console**	Sets console line password
Calgary(config-line)#**logging synchronous**	Returns prompt to same location after info messages interrupt
Calgary(config-line)#**exit**	
Calgary(config)#**int fa 0/0**	
Calgary(config-if)#**ip add 172.16.30.1 255.255.255.0**	Assigns IP address to interface
Calgary(config-if)#**no shut**	Turns interface on
Calgary(config-if)#**exit**	
Calgary(config)#**username Edmonton password academy**	For PPP encapsulation across ISDN (optional)

`Calgary(config)#isdn switch-type basic-ni`	Sets ISDN switch type for all interfaces to match service provider
`Calgary(config)#dialer-list 1 protocol ip permit`	Defines interesting traffic—all IP
`Calgary(config)#ip route 0.0.0.0 0.0.0.0 172.16.20.1`	Creates a static route that will send all traffic not defined in the routing table to the next-hop address of 172.16.20.1
`Calgary(config)#int bri 0/0`	
`Calgary(config-if)#ip add 172.16.20.2 255.255.255.0`	Assigns IP address to interface
`Calgary(config-if)#encap ppp`	Turns on PPP encapsulation
`Calgary(config-if)#ppp authen chap`	Turns on CHAP authentication
`Calgary(config-if)#dialer-group 1`	Assigns traffic from dialer list 1 to this group
`Calgary(config-if)#isdn spid1 51055540000001 5554000`	Assigns SPID 1
`Calgary(config-if)#isdn spid2 51055540010001 5554001`	Assigns SPID 2
`Calgary(config-if)#dialer idle-timeout 60`	Specifies that the interface will disconnect after 60 seconds of no traffic
`Calgary(config-if)#dialer map ip 172.16.20.1 name Edmonton 5551234`	Sets map to find remote router
`Calgary(config-if)#no shut`	
`Calgary(config-if)#`Ctrl z	
`Calgary#copy run start`	Saves configuration to NVRAM

CHAPTER 5

Frame Relay

This chapter provides information and commands concerning the following topics:

- Configuring Frame Relay
  - Setting the encapsulation type
  - Setting the LMI type
  - Setting the DLCI number
  - Configuring a Frame Relay map statement
  - Configuring Frame Relay using subinterfaces
- Verifying Frame Relay
- Troubleshooting Frame Relay

Configuring Frame Relay: Setting the Frame Relay Encapsulation Type

`Router(config)#int s 0/0`	
`Router(config-if)#encapsulation frame-relay`	Turns on Frame Relay encapsulation with the default encapsulation type of **cisco**
or	
`Router(config-if)#encapsulation frame-relay ietf`	Turns on Frame Relay encapsulation with the encapsulation type of **ietf** (RFC 1490). Use the **ietf** encapsulation method if connecting to a non-Cisco router

Configuring Frame Relay: Setting the Frame Relay Encapsulation LMI Type

`Router(config-if)#frame-relay lmi-type {ansi ¦ cisco ¦ q933a}`	Depending on the option you select, this command sets the LMI type to the ANSI standard, the Cisco standard, or the ITU-T Q.933 Annex A standard

NOTE: As of Cisco IOS Software Release 11.2 the LMI type is auto-sensed, making this command optional

Configuring Frame Relay: Setting the Frame Relay DLCI Number

`Router(config-if)#frame-relay interface-dlci 110`	Sets the DLCI number of 110 on the local interface
`Router(config-fr-dlci)#exit`	
`Router(config)#`	

Configuring a Frame Relay Map

`Router(config-if)#frame-relay map ip 192.168.100.1 110 broadcast`	Maps the remote IP address (192.168.100.1) to the local DLCI number (110)
	The optional **broadcast** keyword specifies that broadcasts across IP should be forwarded to this address. This is necessary when using dynamic routing protocols
`Router(config-if)#no frame-relay inverse arp`	Turns off Inverse ARP

NOTE: Cisco routers have Inverse Address Resolution Protocol (ARP) turned on by default. This means that the router will go out and create the mapping for you. If the remote router does not support Inverse ARP, or you want to control broadcast traffic over the permanent virtual circuit (PVC), you must statically set the DLCI/IP mappings and turn off Inverse ARP.

You need to issue the **no frame-relay inverse-arp** command before you issue the **no shutdown** command; otherwise, the interface performs Inverse ARP before you can turn it off.

Configuring a Description of the Interface (Optional)

`Router(config-if)#description Connection to the Branch office`	Optional command to allow you to enter in additional information such as contact name, PVC description, and so on

Configuring Frame Relay Using Subinterfaces

Subinterfaces enable you to solve split-horizon problems and to create multiple PVCs on a single physical connection to the Frame Relay cloud.

`Router(config)#int s 0/0`	
`Router(config-if)#encapsulation frame-relay ietf`	Sets the Frame Relay encapsulation type for all subinterfaces on this interface
`Router(config-if)#frame-relay lmi-type ansi`	Sets the LMI type for all subinterfaces on this interface
`Router(config-if)#no shut`	
`Router(config-if)#interface s 0/0.102 point-to-point`	Creates a point-to-point subinterface numbered 102
`Router(config-subif)#ip address 192.168.10.1 255.255.255.0`	Assigns an IP address to the subinterface
`Router(config-subif)#frame-relay interface-dlci 102`	Assigns a DLCI to the subinterface

`Router(config-subif)#int s 0/0.103 point-to-point`	Creates a point-to-point subinterface numbered 103
`Router(config-subif)#ip address 192.168.20.1 255.255.255.0`	Assigns a IP address to the subinterface
`Router(config-subif)#frame-relay interface-dlci 103`	Assigns a DLCI to the subinterface
`Router(config-subif)#exit`	
`Router(config-if)#exit`	
`Router(config)#`	

NOTE: There are two types of subinterfaces:

- **Point-to-point**, where a single PVC connects one router to another and each subinterface is in its own IP subnet.
- **Multipoint**, where the router is the middle point of a group of routers. All other routers connect to each other through this router and all routers are in the same subnet.

NOTE: Use the **no ip split-horizon** command to turn off split-horizon commands on multipoint interfaces so that remote sites can see each other.

Verifying Frame Relay

`Router#show frame-relay map`	Displays IP/DLCI map entries
`Router#show frame-relay pvc`	Displays status of all PVCs configured
`Router#show frame-relay lmi`	Displays LMI statistics
`Router#clear frame-relay-inarp`	Clears all Inverse ARP entries from the map table

TIP: If the **clear frame-relay-inarp** command does not clear Frame Relay maps, you might need to reload the router.

Troubleshooting Frame Relay

`Router#debug frame-relay lmi`	Used to help determine whether a router and Frame Relay switch are exchanging LMI packets properly

Configuration Example: Frame Relay

Figure 5-1 shows the network topology for the Frame Relay configuration that follows using the commands covered in this chapter.

Figure 5-1   Frame Relay Network

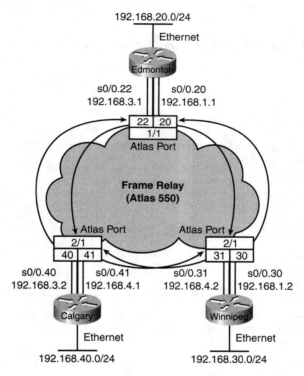

Edmonton Router

router>**en**	
router#**config t**	
router(config)#**host Edmonton**	Sets the host name
Edmonton(config)#**no ip domain-lookup**	Turns off DNS queries so that spelling mistakes will not slow you down

Edmonton(config)#**enable secret cisco**	Sets the encrypted password
Edmonton(config)#**line con 0**	
Edmonton(config-line)#**login**	
Edmonton(config-line)#**password class**	Sets console line password to class
Edmonton(config-line)#**logging synchronous**	Command being entered will be appended to a new line
Edmonton(config-line)#**exit**	
Edmonton(config)#**int fa 0/0**	
Edmonton(config-if)#**ip address 192.168.20.1 255.255.255.0**	Assigns IP address
Edmonton(config-if)#**no shut**	
Edmonton(config-if)#**int s 0/0**	
Edmonton(config-if)#**encapsulation frame-relay**	Turns on Frame Relay encapsulation
Edmonton(config-if)#**no shut**	
Edmonton(config-if)#**int s0/0.20 point-to-point**	Creates subinterface 20
Edmonton(config-subif)#**desc link to Winnipeg router DLCI 20**	
Edmonton(config-subif)#**ip address 192.168.1.1 255.255.255.0**	Assigns an IP address
Edmonton(config-subif)#**frame-relay interface-dlci 20**	Assigns a DLCI number
Edmonton(config-subif)#**interface s 0/0.22**	Creates subinterface 22
Edmonton(config-subif)#**desc link to Calgary router DLCI 22**	
Edmonton(config-subif)#**ip address 192.168.3.1 255.255.255.0**	Assigns an IP address
Edmonton(config-subif)#**frame-relay interface dlci 22**	Assigns a DLCI number

Edmonton(config-subif)#**exit**	
Edmonton(config-if)#**exit**	
Edmonton(config)#**router eigrp 100**	Turns on the EIGRP routing process 100
Edmonton(config-router)#**network 192.168.1.0**	Advertises network 192.168.1.0, which connects to Winnipeg
Edmonton(config-router)#**network 192.168.3.0**	Advertises network 192.168.3.0, which connects to Calgary
Edmonton(config-router)#**network 192.168.20.0**	Advertises network 192.168.20.0, which is directly connected to local FA 0/interface
Edmonton(config-router)#Ctrl z	
Edmonton#**copy run start**	Saves the configuration to NVRAM

Winnipeg Router

router>**en**	
router#**config t**	
router(config)#**host Winnipeg**	Sets the host name
Winnipeg(config)#**no ip domain-lookup**	Turns off DNS queries so that spelling mistakes will not slow you down
Winnipeg(config)#**enable secret cisco**	Sets the encrypted password to **cisco**
Winnipeg(config)#**line con 0**	
Winnipeg(config-line)#**login**	
Winnipeg(config-line)#**password class**	Sets the console line password to **class**

`Winnipeg(config-line)#logging synchronous`	Command being entered will be appended to a new line
`Winnipeg(config-line)#exit`	
`Winnipeg(config)#int fa 0/0`	
`Winnipeg(config-if)#ip address 192.168.30.1 255.255.255.0`	Assigns an IP address
`Winnipeg(config-if)#no shut`	
`Winnipeg(config-if)#int s 0/0`	
`Winnipeg(config-if)#encapsulation frame-relay`	Turns on Frame Relay encapsulation
`Winnipeg(config-if)#no shut`	
`Winnipeg(config-if)#int s0/0.30 point-to-point`	Creates subinterface 30
`Winnipeg(config-subif)#desc link to Edmonton router DLCI 30`	
`Winnipeg(config-subif)#ip address 192.168.1.2 255.255.255.0`	Assigns an IP address
`Winnipeg(config-subif)#frame-relay interface-dlci 30`	Assigns a DLCI number
`Winnipeg(config-subif)#interface s 0/0.31`	Creates subinterface 31
`Winnipeg(config-subif)#desc link to Calgary router DLCI 31`	
`Winnipeg(config-subif)#ip address 192.168.4.2 255.255.255.0`	Assigns an IP address
`Winnipeg(config-subif)#frame-relay interface-dlci 31`	Assigns a DLCI number
`Winnipeg(config-subif)#exit`	
`Winnipeg(config-if)#exit`	
`Winnipeg(config)#router eigrp 100`	Turns on EIGRP routing process 100
`Winnipeg(config-router)#network 192.168.1.0`	Advertises network 192.168.1.0 (to Winnipeg)

`Winnipeg(config-router)#`**`network 192.168.4.0`**	Advertises network to 192.168.4.0 (to Calgary)
`Winnipeg(config-router)#`**`network 192.168.30.0`**	Advertises network 192.168.30.0 directly connected to FA 0/0
`Winnipeg(config-router)#`Ctrl z	
`Winnipeg#`**`copy run start`**	Saves the configuration to NVRAM

Calgary Router

`router>`**`en`**	
`router#`**`config t`**	
`router(config)#`**`host Calgary`**	Sets the host name
`Calgary(config)#`**`no ip domain-lookup`**	Turns off DNS queries so that spelling mistakes will not slow you down
`Calgary(config)#`**`enable secret cisco`**	Sets the encrypted password to **cisco**
`Calgary(config)#`**`line con 0`**	
`Calgary(config-line)#`**`login`**	
`Calgary(config-line)#`**`password class`**	Sets the console line password to **class**
`Calgary(config-line)#`**`logging synchronous`**	Command being entered will be appended to a new line
`Calgary(config-line)#`**`exit`**	
`Calgary(config)#`**`int fa 0/0`**	
`Calgary(config-if)#`**`ip address 192.168.40.1 255.255.255.0`**	Assigns an IP address
`Calgary(config-if)#`**`no shut`**	
`Calgary(config-if)#`**`int s 0/0`**	

`Calgary(config-if)#encapsulation frame-relay`	Turns on Frame Relay encapsulation
`Calgary(config-if)#no shut`	
`Calgary(config-if)#int s0/0.40 point-to-point`	Creates subinterface 40
`Calgary(config-subif)#desc link to Edmonton router DLCI 40`	
`Calgary(config-subif)#ip address 192.168.3.2 255.255.255.0`	Assigns an IP address
`Calgary(config-subif)#frame-relay interface-dlci 40`	Assigns a DLCI number
`Calgary(config-subif)#interface s 0/0.41`	Creates subinterface 41
`Calgary(config-subif)#desc link to Winnipeg router DLCI 41`	
`Calgary(config-subif)#ip address 192.168.4.1 255.255.255.0`	Assigns an IP address
`Calgary(config-subif)#frame-relay interface-dlci 41`	Assigns a DLCI number
`Calgary(config-subif)#exit`	
`Calgary(config-if)#exit`	
`Calgary(config)#router eigrp 100`	Turns on EIGRP routing process 100
`Calgary(config-router)#network 192.168.3.0`	Advertises the network to Winnipeg
`Calgary(config-router)#network 192.168.4.0`	Advertises the network to Calgary
`Calgary(config-router)#network 192.168.40.0`	Advertises the local fa 0/0 network
`Calgary(config-router)#`Ctrl z	
`Calgary#copy run start`	Saves the configuration to NVRAM

CHAPTER 6

Introduction to Network Administration

This chapter provides information and commands concerning the following topics:

- Configuring Simple Network Management Protocol (SNMP)
- Configuring Syslog

Configuring SNMP

`Router(config)#snmp-server community academy ro`	Sets a read-only (**ro**) community string called **academy**
`Router(config)#snmp-server community academy rw`	Sets a read-write (**rw**) community string called **academy**
`Router(config)#snmp-server location 2nd Floor IDF`	Defines an SNMP string that describes the physical location of the SNMP server
`Router(config)#snmp-server contact Scott Empson 555-5236`	Defines an SNMP string that describes the sysContact information

NOTE: A community string is like a password. In the case of the first command, the community string grants you access to SNMP.

Configuring Syslog

`Router(config)#logging on`	Enables logging to all supported destinations
`Router(config)#logging 192.168.10.53`	Logging messages will be sent to a syslog server host at address 192.168.10.53

`Router(config)#logging sysadmin`	Logging messages will be sent to a syslog server host named sysadmin
`Router(config)#logging trap x`	Sets the syslog server logging level to value x, where x is a number between 0 and 7 or a word defining the level. The table that follows provides more details
`Router(config)#service timestamps log datetime`	Syslog messages will now have a time stamp included

There are eight levels of severity in logging messages, as follows:

0	Emergencies	System is unusable
1	Alerts	Immediate action needed
2	Critical	Critical conditions
3	Errors	Error conditions
4	Warnings	Warning conditions
5	Notifications	Normal but significant conditions
6	Informational	Informational messages (default level)
7	Debugging	Debugging messages

Setting a level means you will get that level and everything below it. Level 6 means you will receive level 6 and 7 messages. Level 4 means you will get levels 4 through 7.

PART V

Appendixes

Subnetting

Class A–E Addresses

Class	Leading Bit Pattern	First Octet in Decimal	Notes
A	0xxxxxxx	0–127	0 is invalid 127 reserved for loopback testing
B	10xxxxxx	128–191	
C	110xxxxx	192–223	
D	1110xxxx	224–239	Reserved for multicasting
E	1111xxxx	240–255	Reserved for future use/testing

Formulae	
2^N Where N is equal to number of bits borrowed	Number of total subnets created
$2^N - 2$	Number of valid subnets created
2^H Where H is equal to number of host bits	Number of total hosts per subnet
$2^H - 2$	Number of valid hosts per subnet

Class A Address	N	H	H	H
Class B Address	N	N	H	H
Class C Address	N	N	N	H

N = Network bits
H = Host bits
All 0s in host portion = Network or subnetwork address
All 1s in host portion = Broadcast address
Combination of 1s and 0s in host portion = Valid host address

Converting Between Decimal Numbers and Binary

In any given octet of an IP address, the 8 bits can be defined as follows:

2^7	2^6	2^5	2^4	2^3	2^2	2^1	2^0
128	64	32	16	8	4	2	1

To convert a decimal number into binary, you must turn on the bits (make them a 1) that would add up to that number, as follows:

    187 = 10111011 = 128+32+16+8+2+1
    224 = 11100000 = 128+64+32

To convert a binary number into decimal, you must add the bits that have been turned on (the 1s), as follows:

    10101010 = 128+32+8+2 = 170
    11110000 = 128+64+32+16 = 240

The IP address 138.101.114.250 is represented in binary as:

    10001010.01100101.01110010.11111010

The subnet mask of 255.255.255.192 is represented in binary as:

    11111111.11111111.11111111.11000000

Subnetting a Class C Network Using Binary

You have a Class C address of 192.168.100.0 /24. You need nine subnets. What is the IP plan of network numbers, broadcast numbers, and valid host numbers? What is the subnet mask needed for this plan?

You cannot use N bits, only H bits. Therefore, ignore 192.168.100. These numbers cannot change.

Step 1   Determine how many H bits you need to borrow to create nine valid subnets.

$2^N - 2 \geq 9$

N = 4, so you need to borrow 4 H bits and turn them into N bits.

Start with 8 H bits	HHHHHHHH
Borrow 4 bits	NNNN HHHH

Step 2   Determine the first valid subnet in binary.

0001HHHH	Cannot use subnet 0000 because it is invalid. Therefore, you must start with the bit pattern of 0001
0001**0000**	All 0s in host portion = subnetwork number
0001**0001**	First valid host number
.	
.	
.	
0001**1110**	Last valid host number
0001**1111**	All 1s in host portion = broadcast number

Step 3   Convert binary to decimal.

00010000 = 16	Subnetwork number
00010001 = 17	First valid host number
.	
.	
.	
00011110 = 30	Last valid host number
00011111 = 31	All 1s in host portion = broadcast number

Step 4   Determine the second valid subnet in binary.

0010HHHH	0010 = 2 in binary = second valid subnet
0010**0000**	All 0s in host portion = subnetwork number
0010**0001**	First valid host number
.	
.	
.	
0010**1110**	Last valid host number
0010**1111**	All 1s in host portion = broadcast number

Step 5   Convert binary to decimal.

00100000 = 16	Subnetwork number
00100001 = 17	First valid host number
.	
.	
.	
00101110 = 30	Last valid host number
00101111 = 31	All 1s in host portion = broadcast number

Step 6   Create IP plan table.

Valid Subnet	Network Number	Range of Valid Hosts	Broadcast Number
1	16	17–30	31
2	32	33–46	47
3	48	49–62	63

Notice a pattern? Counting by 16.

Step 7   Verify pattern in binary (third valid subnet in binary used here).

0011HHHH	Third valid subnet
00110000 = **48**	Subnetwork number
00110001 = **49**	First valid host number
.	
.	
.	
00111110 = **62**	Last valid host number
00111111 = **63**	Broadcast number

Step 8   Finish IP plan table.

Subnet	Network Address (0000)	Range of Valid Hosts (0001–1110)	Broadcast Address (1111)
0 (0000) invalid	~~192.168.100.0~~	~~192.168.100.1~~ – ~~192.168.100.14~~	~~192.168.100.15~~
1 (0001)	192.168.100.16	192.168.100.17 – 192.168.100.30	192.168.100.31
2 (0010)	192.168.100.32	192.168.100.33 – 192.168.100.46	192.168.100.47
3 (0011)	192.168.100.48	192.168.100.49 – 192.168.100.62	192.168.100.63
4 (0100)	192.168.100.64	192.168.100.65 – 192.168.100.78	192.168.100.79
5 (0101)	192.168.100.80	192.168.100.81 – 192.168.100.94	192.168.100.95
6 (0110)	192.168.100.96	192.168.100.97 – 192.168.100.110	192.168.100.111
7 (0111)	192.168.100.112	192.168.100.113 – 192.168.100.126	192.168.100.127
8 (1000)	192.168.100.128	192.168.100.129 – 192.168.100.142	192.168.100.143
9 (1001)	192.168.100.144	192.168.100.145 – 192.168.100.158	192.168.100.159
10 (1010)	192.168.100.160	192.168.100.161 – 192.168.100.174	192.168.100.175
11 (1011)	192.168.100.176	192.168.100.177 – 192.168.100.190	192.168.100.191
12 (1100)	192.168.100.192	192.168.100.193 – 192.168.100.206	192.168.100.207
13 (1101)	192.168.100.208	192.168.100.209 – 192.168.100.222	192.168.100.223

14 (1110)	192.168.100.**224**	192.168.100.**225**– 192.168.100.**238**	192.168.100.**239**
15 (1111) invalid	~~192.168.100.240~~	~~192.168.100.241~~– ~~192.168.100.254~~	~~192.168.100.255~~
Quick Check	**Always an even number**	**First valid host is always an odd #** **Last valid host is always even #**	**Always an odd number**

Use any nine subnets—the rest are for future growth

Step 9   Calculate subnet mask.

The default subnet mask for a Class C network is as follows:

Decimal	Binary
255.255.255.0	11111111.11111111.11111111.00000000

1 = Network or subnetwork bit
0 = Host bit

You borrowed 4 bits; therefore, the new subnet mask is the following:

11111111.11111111.11111111.**1111**0000	255.255.255.**240**

NOTE: You subnet a Class B or a Class A network with exactly the same steps as for a Class C network; the only difference is that you start with more H bits.

Subnetting a Class B Network Using Binary

You have a Class B address of 172.16.0.0 /16. You need nine subnets. What is the IP plan of network numbers, broadcast numbers, and valid host numbers? What is the subnet mask needed for this plan?

You cannot use N bits, only H bits. Therefore, ignore 172.16. These numbers cannot change.

Step 1   Determine how many H bits you need to borrow to create nine valid subnets.

$$2^N - 2 \geq 9$$

N = 4, so you need to borrow 4 H bits and turn them into N bits.

Start with 16 H bits	HHHHHHHHHHHHHHHH (Remove the decimal point for now)
Borrow 4 bits	NNNNHHHHHHHHHHHH

Step 2   Determine the first valid subnet in binary (without using decimal points).

0001HHHHHHHHHHHH	
0001000000000000	Subnet number
0001000000000001	First valid host
.	
.	
.	
0001111111111110	Last valid host
0001111111111111	Broadcast number

Step 3   Convert binary to decimal (replacing the decimal point in the binary numbers).

00010000.00000000 = 16.0	Subnetwork number
00010000.00000001 = 16.1	First valid host number
.	
.	
.	
00011111.11111110 = 31.254	Last valid host number
00011111.11111111 = 31.255	Broadcast number

Step 4   Determine the second valid subnet in binary (without using decimal points).

0010HHHHHHHHHHHH	
0010000000000000	Subnet number
0010000000000001	First valid host
.	
.	

.	
0010**111111111110**	Last valid host
0010**111111111111**	Broadcast number

Step 5   Convert binary to decimal (replacing the decimal point in the binary numbers).

00100000.00000000 = 32.0	Subnetwork number
00100000.00000001 = 32.1	First valid host number
.	
.	
.	
00101111.11111110 = 47.254	Last valid host number
00101111.11111111 = 47.255	Broadcast number

Step 6   Create IP plan table.

Valid Subnet	Network Number	Range of Valid Hosts	Broadcast Number
1	16.0	16.1–31.254	31.255
2	32.0	32.1–47.254	47.255
3	48.0	48.1–63.254	63.255

Notice a pattern? Counting by 16.

Step 7   Verify pattern in binary (third valid subnet in binary used here).

0011HHHHHHHHHHHH	Third valid subnet
00110000.00000000 = 48.0	Subnetwork number
00110000.00000001 = 48.1	First valid host number
.	
.	
.	
00111111.11111110 = 63.254	Last valid host number
00111111.11111111 = 63.255	Broadcast number

Step 8   Finish IP plan table.

Subnet	Network Address (0000)	Range of Valid Hosts (0001–1110)	Broadcast Address (1111)
0 (0000) invalid	~~172.16.**0.0**~~	~~172.16.**0.1**–172.16.**15.254**~~	~~172.16.**15.255**~~
1 (0001)	172.16.**16.0**	172.16.**16.1**–172.16.**31.254**	172.16.**31.255**
2 (0010)	172.16.**32.0**	172.16.**32.1**–172.16.**47.254**	172.16.**47.255**
3 (0011)	172.16.**48.0**	172.16.**48.1**–172.16.**63.254**	172.16.**63.255**
4 (0100)	172.16.**64.0**	172.16.**64.1**–172.16.**79.254**	172.16.**79.255**
5 (0101)	172.16.**80.0**	172.16.**80.1**–172.16.**95.254**	172.16.**95.255**
6 (0110)	172.16.**96.0**	172.16.**96.1**–172.16.**111.254**	172.16.**111.255**
7 (0111)	172.16.**112.0**	172.16.**112.1**–172.16.**127.254**	172.16.**127.255**
8 (1000)	172.16.**128.0**	172.16.**128.1**–172.16.**143.254**	172.16.**143.255**
9 (1001)	172.16.**144.0**	172.16.**144.1**–172.16.**159.254**	172.16.**159.255**
10 (1010)	172.16.**160.0**	172.16.**160.1**–172.16.**175.254**	172.16.**175.255**
11 (1011)	172.16.**176.0**	172.16.**176.1**–172.16.**191.254**	172.16.**191.255**
12 (1100)	172.16.**192.0**	172.16.**192.1**–172.16.**207.254**	172.16.**207.255**
13 (1101)	172.16.**208.0**	172.16.**208.1**–172.16.**223.254**	172.16.**223.255**
14 (1110)	172.16.**224.0**	172.16.**224.1**–172.16.**239.254**	172.16.**239.255**
15 (1111) invalid	~~172.16.**240.0**~~	~~172.16.**240.1**–172.16.**255.254**~~	~~172.16.**255.255**~~
Quick Check	**Always in form even #.0**	**First valid host is always even #.1** **Last valid host is always odd #.254**	**Always odd #.255**

Use any nine subnets—the rest are for future growth.

Step 9   Calculate the subnet mask.

The default subnet mask for a Class B network is as follows:

Decimal	Binary
255.255.0.0	11111111.11111111.00000000.00000000

1 = Network or subnetwork bit
0 = Host bit

You borrowed 4 bits; therefore, the new subnet mask is the following:

11111111.11111111.**1111**0000.00000000	255.255.**240**.0

The Enhanced Bob Maneuver for Subnetting (or How to Subnet Anything in Under a Minute)

Legend has it that once upon a time a networking instructor named Bob taught a class of students a method of subnetting any address using a special chart. This was known as the Bob Maneuver. These students, being the smart type that networking students usually are, added a row to the top of the chart and the Enhanced Bob Maneuver was born. The chart and instructions on how to use it follow. With practice, you should be able to subnet any address and come up with an IP plan in under a minute. After all, it's *just* math!

The Bob of the Enhanced Bob Maneuver was really a manager/instructor at SHL. He taught this maneuver to Bruce, who taught it to Chad Klymchuk. Chad and a coworker named Troy added the top line of the chart, enhancing it. Chad was first my instructor in Microsoft, then my coworker here at NAIT, and now is one of my Academy Instructors—I guess I am now his boss. And the circle is complete.

The Enhanced Bob Maneuver

	192	224	240	248	252	254	255	Subnet Mask
128	64	32	16	8	4	2	1	Target Number
8	7	6	5	4	3	2	1	Bit Place
	126	62	30	14	6	4	N/A	Number of Valid Subnets

Suppose that you have a Class C network and you need nine subnets.

1. On the bottom line (Number of Valid Subnets), move from *right* to *left* and find the closest number that is *bigger* than or *equal* to what you need:

   Nine subnets—move to 14.

2. From that number (14), move up to the line called Bit Place.

Above 14 is bit place 4.

3. The dark line is called the *high-order line*. If you cross the line, you have to reverse direction

    You were moving right to left; now you have to move from left to right.

4. Go to the line called Target Number. Counting *from the left*, move over the number of spaces that the bit place number tells you

    Starting on 128, moving 4 places takes you to 16.

5. This target number is what you need to count by, starting at 0, and going until you hit 255 or greater. Stop before you get to 256:

    0

    16

    32

    48

    64

    80

    96

    112

    128

    144

    160

    176

    192

    208

    224

    240

    ~~256~~ Stop—too far!

6. These numbers are your network numbers. Expand to finish your plan.

Network #	Range of Valid Hosts	Broadcast Number
0 (invalid)	1–14	15
16	17–30 (17 is 1 more than network # 30 is 1 less than broadcast#)	31 (1 less than next network #)
32	33–46	47
48	49–62	63
64	65–78	79
80	81–94	95
96	97–110	111
112	113–126	127
128	129–142	143
144	145–158	159
160	161–174	175
176	177–190	191
192	193–206	207
208	209–222	223
224	225–238	239
240 (invalid)	241–254	255

Notice that there are 14 subnets created from .16 to .224.

7. Go back to the Enhanced Bob Maneuver chart and look above your target number to the top line. The number above your target number is your subnet mask

Above 16 is 240. Because you started with a Class C network, the new subnet mask is 255.255.255.240.

APPENDIX B

VLSM

Variable-length subnet masking (VLSM) is the more realistic way of subnetting a network to make for the most efficient use of all of the bits.

Remember that when you perform classful (or what I sometimes call classical) subnetting, all subnets have the same number of hosts because they all use the same subnet mask. This leads to inefficiencies. For example, if you borrow 4 bits on a Class C network, you end up with 14 valid subnets of 14 valid hosts. A serial link to another router only needs 2 hosts, but with classical subnetting you end up wasting 12 of those hosts. Even with the ability to use NAT and private addresses, where you should never run out of addresses ever in a network design, you still want to ensure that the IP plan that you create is as efficient as possible. This is where VLSM comes in to play.

VLSM is the process of "subnetting a subnet" and using different subnet masks for different networks in your IP plan. What you have to remember is that you need to make sure that there is no overlap in any of the addresses.

IP Subnet Zero

When you work with classical subnetting, you always have to eliminate the subnets that contain either all zeros or all ones in the subnet portion. Hence, you always used the formula $2^N - 2$ to define the number of valid subnets created. However, Cisco devices can use those subnets, as long as the command **ip subnet-zero** is in the configuration. This command is on by default in Cisco IOS Software Release 12.0 and later; if it was turned off for some reason, however, you can re-enable it by using the following command:

```
Router(config)#ip subnet-zero
```

Now you can use the formula 2^N rather than $2^N - 2$.

2^N	Number of total subnets created	
~~$2^N - 2$~~	~~Number of valid subnets created~~	No longer needed because you have the **ip subnet-zero** command enabled
2^H	Number of total hosts per subnet	
$2^H - 2$	Number of valid hosts per subnet	

PART V APPENDIXES

VLSM Example

You follow the same steps in performing VLSM as you did when performing classical subnetting.

Consider Figure B-1 as you work through an example.

Figure B-1   Sample Network Needing a VLSM Address Plan

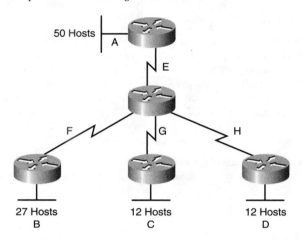

A Class C network—192.168.100.0/24—is assigned. You need to create an IP plan for this network using VLSM.

Once again, you cannot use the N bits—192.168.100. You can use only the H bits. Therefore, ignore the N bits, because they cannot change!

The steps to create an IP plan using VLSM for the network illustrated in Figure B-1 are as follows:

Step 1   Determine how many H bits will be needed to satisfy the *largest* network.

Step 2   Pick a subnet for the largest network to use.

Step 3   Pick the next largest network to work with.

Step 4   Pick the third largest network to work with.

Step 5   Determine network numbers for serial links.

The remainder of the chapter details what is involved with each step of the process.

Step 1 Determine How Many H Bits Will Be Needed to Satisfy the *Largest* Network

A is the largest network with 50 hosts. Therefore, you need to know how many H bits will be needed:

$2^H - 2$ = Number of valid hosts per subnet
$2^H - 2 \geq 50$
$H = 6$

You need 6 H bits to satisfy the requirements of Network A.

If you need 6 H bits and you started with 8 N bits, you are left with $8 - 6 = 2$ N bits to create subnets:

Started with: NNNNNNNN (these are the 8 bits in the fourth octet)
Now have: NNHHHHHH

All subnetting will now have to start at this reference point, to satisfy the requirements of Network A.

Step 2 Pick a Subnet for the Largest Network to Use

You have 2 N bits to work with, leaving you with 2^N or 2^2 or 4 subnets to work with:

NN = 00HHHHHH (The Hs = The 6 H bits you need for Network A)
01HHHHHH
10HHHHHH
11HHHHHH

If you add all zeros to the H bits, you are left with the network numbers for the four subnets:

00000000 = .0
01000000 = .64
10000000 = .128
11000000 = .192

All of these subnets will have the same subnet mask, just like in classful subnetting.

Two borrowed H bits means a subnet mask of:

11111111.11111111.11111111.11000000

or

255.255.255.192

or

/26

The /x notation represents how to show different subnet masks when using VLSM.

/8 means that the first 8 bits of the address are network, the remaining 24 bits are H bits

/24 means that the first 24 bits are network, the last 8 are host—this is either a traditional default Class C address, or a traditional Class A network that has borrowed 16 bits, or even a traditional Class B network that has borrowed 8 bits!

Pick *one* of these subnets to use for Network A. The rest of the networks will have to use the other three subnets.

For purposes of this example, pick the .64 network.

00000000 =	.0	
~~01000000 =~~	~~.64~~	Network A
10000000 =	.128	
11000000 =	.192	

Step 3 Pick the Next Largest Network to Work With
Network B = 27 hosts

Determine the number of H bits needed for this network:

$$2^H - 2 \geq 27$$
$$H = 5$$

You need 5 H bits to satisfy the requirements of Network B.

You started with a pattern of 2 N bits and 6 H bits for Network A. You have to maintain that pattern.

Pick one of the remaining /26 networks to work with Network B.

For purposes of this example, select the .128/26 network:

10000000

But you need only 5 H bits, not 6. Therefore, you are left with:

10N00000

where:

10 represents the original pattern of subnetting.
N represents the extra bit we have.
00000 represents the 5 H bits you need for Network B.

Because you have this extra bit, you can create two smaller subnets from the original subnet:

10000000
10100000

Converted to decimal, these subnets are as follows:

10000000 =.128
10100000 =.160

You have now subnetted a subnet! This is the basis of VLSM.

Each of these sub-subnets will have a new subnet mask. The original subnet mask of /24 was changed into /26 for Network A. You then take one of these /26 networks and break it into two /27 networks:

10**000000** and 10**100000** both have 3 N bits and 5 H bits.

The mask now equals:

11111111.11111111.11111111.11100000

or

255.255.255.224

or

/27

Pick one of these new sub-subnets for Network B:

10**000000** /27 = Network B

Use the remaining sub-subnet for future growth, or you can break it down further if needed.

You want to make sure the addresses are not overlapping with each other. So go back to the original table.

00**000000** =	.0/26	
~~01**000000** =~~	~~.64/26~~	Network A
10**000000** =	.128/26	
11**000000** =	.192/26	

You can now break the .128/26 network into two smaller /27 networks and assign Network B.

00**000000** =	.0/26	
~~01**000000** =~~	~~.64/26~~	Network A
~~10**000000** =~~	~~.128/26~~	Cannot use because it has been subnetted
~~10**000000** =~~	~~.128/27~~	Network B
10**100000** =	160/27	
11**000000** =	.192/26	

The remaining networks are still available to be assigned to networks, or subnetted further for better efficiency.

Step 4 Pick the Third Largest Network to Work With

Networks C and Network D = 12 hosts each

Determine the number of H bits needed for these networks:

$$2^H - 2 \geq 12$$
$$H = 4$$

You need 4 H bits to satisfy the requirements of Network C and Network D.

You started with a pattern of 2 N bits and 6 H bits for Network A. You have to maintain that pattern.

You now have a choice as to where to put these networks. You could go to a different /26 network, or you could go to a /27 network and try to fit them into there.

For the purposes of this example, select the other /27 network—.160/27:

10100000 (The 1 in the third bit place is no longer bold, because it is part of the N bits.)

But you only need 4 H bits, not 5. Therefore you are left with:

101N0000

where:

10 represents the original pattern of subnetting.
N represents the extra bit you have.
00000 represents the 5 H bits you need for Network B.

Because you have this extra bit, you can create two smaller subnets from the original subnet:

101**00000**
101**10000**

Converted to decimal, these subnets are as follows:

101**00000** = .160
101**10000** = .176

These new sub-subnets will now have new subnet masks. Each sub-subnet now has 4 N bits and 4 H bits, so their new masks will be:

11111111.11111111.11111111.11110000

or

255.255.255.240

or

/28

Pick one of these new sub-subnets for Network C and one for Network D.

00000000 =	.0/26	
~~01000000 =~~	~~.64/26~~	Network A
~~10000000 =~~	~~.128/26~~	Cannot use because it has been subnetted
~~10000000 =~~	~~.128/27~~	Network B
~~10100000 =~~	~~160/27~~	Cannot use because it has been subnetted
10100000	160/28	Network C
10110000	176/28	Network D
11000000 =	.192/26	

You have now used two of the original four subnets to satisfy the requirements of four networks. Now all you need to do is determine the network numbers for the serial links between the routers.

Step 5 Determine Network Numbers for Serial Links

Serial links between routers all have the same property in that they only need two addresses in a network—one for each router interface.

Determine the number of H bits needed for these networks:

$$2^H - 2 \geq 2$$
$$H = 2$$

You need 2 H bits to satisfy the requirements of Networks E, F, G, and H.

You have two of the original subnets left to work with.

For purposes of this example, select the .0/26 network:

00000000

But you need only 2 H bits, not 6. Therefore, you are left with:

00NNNN**00**

where:

00 represents the original pattern of subnetting.
NNNN represents the extra bits you have.
00 represents the 2 H bits you need for the serial links.

Because you have 4 **N** bits, you can create 16 sub-subnets from the original subnet:

000000**00** = .0/30
000001**00** = .4/30
000010**00** = .8/30
000011**00** = .12/30

000100**00** = .16/30
.
.
.
001110**00** = .56/30
001111**00** = .60/30

You need only four of them. You can hold the rest for future expansion, or recombine them for a new, larger subnet:

000100**00** = .16/30
.
.
.
001110**00** = .56/30
001111**00** = .60/30

These can all be recombined into the following:

00010000 = .16/28

Going back to the original table, you now have the following:

00000000 =	.0/26	Cannot use because it has been subnetted
00000000 =	.0/30	Network E
00000100 =	.4/30	Network F
00001000 =	.8/30	Network G
00001100 =	.12/30	Network H
00010000 =	.16/28	Future growth
01000000 =	.64/26	Network A
10000000 =	.128/26	Cannot use because it has been subnetted
10000000 =	.128/27	Network B
10100000 =	160/27	Cannot use because it has been subnetted
10100000	160/28	Network C
10110000	176/28	Network D
11000000 =	.192/26	Future growth

Looking at the plan, you can see that no number is used twice. You have now created an IP plan for the network, and have made the plan as efficient as possible, wasting no addresses in the serial links and leaving room for future growth. This is the power of VLSM!